Healing *Chronic* Candida

COOKBOOK

Diet Tips, Meal Plans, and 125+ Delicious Low-Carb and Paleo Friendly Recipes

CYNTHIA PERKINS, M.ED.

Basic Health
PUBLICATIONS, INC.

The information contained in this book is based upon the research and personal and professional experiences of the author. It is not intended as a substitute for consulting with your physician or other health-care provider. Any attempt to diagnose and treat an illness should be done under the direction of a health-care professional.

If you are on medication for diabetes or heart disease, and are going low-carb for the first time, then an adjustment in medication may be needed. So it is important to discuss these changes in diet with your physician. If you are pregnant, nursing, or engaging in a competitive sport competition, this is not the best time to begin a very low-carb diet. If you have been low-carb before becoming pregnant or nursing or engaging in competition, then your body will already be adapted.

The publisher does not advocate the use of any particular health-care protocol but believes the information in this book should be available to the public. The publisher and author are not responsible for any adverse effects or consequences resulting from the use of the suggestions, preparations, or procedures discussed in this book. Should the reader have any questions concerning the appropriateness of any procedures or preparation mentioned, the author and the publisher strongly suggest consulting a professional health-care advisor.

Turner Publishing Company
Nashville, TN
www.turnerpublishing.com

Library of Congress Cataloging-in-Publication Data is available through the Library of Congress.

Interior design: Gary A. Rosenberg
Cover design: Maddie Cothren

Printed in the United States of America

10   9   8   7   6   5   4   3   2   1

Contents

Paleo for Candida Basics Review, 1

Designing Your Individualized Paleo for Candida Plan, 5

Paleo for Candida Breakfast Ideas, 14

Tips for Staying on Track, 17

What About Those Other Paleo Cookbooks?, 40

Gauging Your Carb Intake and Other Things to Consider, 44

Miscellaneous Tidbits, 59

Paleo for Candida at a Glance, 62

Sample Meal Plans, 64

MAIN COURSE MEALS

Basic Roasted Turkey Breast, 69

Baked Chicken Tenders, 70

Fresh Chicken Salad Medley, 71

Pasta-Free Spaghetti in Meat Sauce, 72

Avocado and Hard-Boiled Egg Sandwich, 73

Meatza Pizza Pie, 74

Mustard and Herb Chicken Thighs, 75

Basic Bunless Burger, 76

Shepherd's Pie, 77

Lemon & Herb Chicken, 78

Beef & Veggie Wraps, 78

Aromatic Roasted Pheasant with Carrots and Celery, 79

Savory Slow-Cooked Brisket, 80

Jalapeño and Guacamole Burger, 80

Salmon Patties, 81

Southwestern Turkey Burger, 82

Simple Roast Duck, 82

Crock Pot Stew, 83

Seared Duck Breast, 84

All the Fixins Bison Burger, 84

Simple Steak Salad, 85

Spicy Green Beans and Ground Beef, 86

Broiled Hot Dogs with Fried Cabbage, 86

Ground Beef or Bison with Stir Fried Cabbage, 87

Pepper and Spinach Egg Scramble, 88

Caveman's Palate Meat Loaf, 89

Turkey Loaf, 90

Holiday Kraut & Dogs Casserole, 90

Scrambled Eggs with Cabbage and Olives, 91

Simple Roast with Vegetables, 92

Easy Minute Steaks with Mixed Peppers, 92

Baked Chicken Breast with California Blend Vegetables, 93

Chicken Salad Supreme, 94

Mexican Paleo Wrap, 94

Hoagie-less Sausage with Peppers and Onions, 95

Fast and Easy Paleo Pizza, 96

Pan-Roasted Lamb Chops with Herbs, 97

Crustless Quiche with Sausage and Veggies, 98

Mouth Watering Barbecue Ribs, 99

Leg of Lamb Roast with Celery, 100

Fajita Bowl, 101

Savory Paleo Meatballs, 102

Beef Stuffed Cabbage Rolls, 103

Homemade Jerky, 104

Quick and Simple Paleo Omelet, 106

Cornish Hen and Vegetables, 107

Pasta-Free Lasagna, 108

Zucchini Noodle and Sausage Casserole, 110

Baked Salmon in Lemon and Garlic Butter, 111

Bison and Cucumber Salad, 112

SIDE DISHES, SOUPS, AND SAUCES

Cauliflower Rice, 113

Zucchini Noodles, 114

Garlic Roasted Broccoli and/or Cauliflower, 115

Spicy Guacamole, 116

Garlic Flavored Brussels Sprouts, 116

Cabbage in Olive Oil, 117

Cinnamon Cabbage, 118

Lemon & Almond Green Bean Salad, 118

Herbed Kale Salad, 119

Refreshing Cucumber and Avocado Salad, 120

Basic Dressing, 121

Tangy Cucumbers, 122

Green Beans in Herbs, 122

Quick and Simple Sautéed Spinach, 123

Chunky Celery Soup, 124

Simple Zucchini Soup, 124

Cream of Broccoli Soup, 125

Rich and Creamy Cauliflower Soup, 126

Mock Mashed Potatoes, 127

I'm in Nirvana Sweet Potato, 128

Celery Sticks Snackers, 130

Oven Roasted Asparagus, 131

Cynthia's Barbecue Sauce, 132

Sweet or Spicy Butter Balls, 132

Holiday Cranberry Sauce, 133

Roasted Zucchini & Yellow Squash, 134

DESSERTS

Dairy-Free Whipped Cream, 135

Pears and Raspberries, 136

The Real Deal Whipped Cream, 137

Cinnamon Baked Pears with Pecans, 138

Banana Bites, 139

Spiced Peaches and Cream Paradise, 141

Baked Apple Slices with Chestnuts, 142

Vanilla Almond Butter, 142

Mixed Berries and Nuts, 143

Sunflower Macaroons, 144

Cherries Drizzled in Almond Butter, 145

Strawberries & Cream, 146

Dipped Dates, 147

Peach Crumble, 148

Nutty Crust, 149

All-Purpose No-Bake Thumbprint Cookies, 150

Pumpkin Pie Mousse, 152

Basic Fruit Salad, 153

Strawberry and Banana Split Parfait, 154

Paleo Approved Candies
  Lemon Drops, 155
  Cinnamon Drops, 156
  Vanilla Drops, 156
  Macadamia Cremes, 156
  Almond Cremes, 157
  Maple Leaves, 157
  Options for All the Coconut
    Candy Recipes, 158
Mini Blueberry Cheesecakes, 159
Raspberry Cobbler, 160
Nuts and Cream, 160
Simply Sautéed Fruit, 161
Chestnut Puree, 162
Gesztenyepure (Hungarian
  Chestnut Puree), 163
Coconut Pops, 163

Vanilla Bean Banana "Ice Cream," 164
Pistachio "Ice Cream," 166
Bananacicle, 166
"Ice Cream" Bites, 167
Pumpkin and Pecan Ice Cream, 168
Frozen Fruit Bowl, 169
Vanilla Pudding, 170
Carob Cream, 171
Any Occasion Fudge, 172
Basic Crust, 174
Classic Apple Pie, 175
All Purpose Carrot Cake, 176
Easy Bake Cookies, 178
Cream Cheese Frosting, 180

BEVERAGES AND SMOOTHIES

Blueberry Smoothie, 181
Strawberry & Coconut Milk
  Smoothie, 182
Peaches & Almond Milk
  Smoothie, 183
Cucumber Splash, 184

Basic Green Smoothie, 184
Tis the Season Smoothie, 185
Sparkling Lemonade, 185
Holiday Nog, 186
Herbal Iced Tea, 187

Carb Charts, 189
Resources, 196
References, 199
Index, 201

Paleo for Candida Basics Review

This cookbook serves as a companion to *Healing Chronic Candida: A Holistic, Natural, and Comprehensive Approach*, my first book in this series. In *Healing Chronic Candida*, we learned that diet is the most critical element of the healing journey. It is the foundation on which everything else is built and will greatly influence each aspect of recovery. Without these changes in diet, you aren't likely to see significant or long-term improvements, regardless of what other steps are taken. Therefore, having an abundance of tasty recipes and meal plans at your fingertips is essential to support you in this process.

To review, it is vital to eat a diet that cuts off the food source for candida and other pathogenic microbes, and their ability to morph into hyphal form and construct biofilms. We also want to choose foods that promote the right pH level, as a gut that is too alkaline encourages overgrowth and morphogenesis of candida, as well as other pathogens; and a body that is too acidic can lead to a wide array of problems as well like osteoporosis, kidney disease, and more. Our diet needs to be rich in foods that will replenish nutrients that may be deficient, support the immune system, adrenal glands, and gut health, enhance neurotransmitter production and function, restore balance to brain chemistry and the endocrine system, reduce sympathetic nervous system activity, and be free of substances that impair immunity, disrupt brain chemistry and endocrine function, inhibit the parasympathetic nervous system, degrade the integrity of the gut, and deplete the adrenal glands and nutrient levels.

When we eat the proper diet, we inhibit candida's ability to grow, morph, communicate, form biofilms, and spread to other areas of the body, eliminate cravings for sugar and carbs, support gut health, reduce sympathetic dominance and enhance our body's ability to fight off candida and other microbes, all of which leads to a lower level of overgrowth, a reduction in symptoms and a more positive response to treatment. Not only that, you'll also provide yourself with protection from other more serious conditions like depression, anxiety disorders and other mental health issues, insulin resistance, type 2 diabetes, obesity, cancer, heart disease, Alzheimer's and much more, which are all linked directly to the consumption of sugar and carbs.

We also learned that the diet that helps us achieve these goals most successfully is a low-carb version of the paleo diet, which in this case, we will call Paleo for Candida Diet, because the paleo diet is the diet that all human beings are genetically designed to eat. Foods that promote candida overgrowth or other pathogenic microbes, impair immunity, degrade the gut, deplete nutrients, create an imbalance in pH, and foster addiction to sugar and carbs are just naturally absent in a low-carb paleo diet. As suggested in *Healing Chronic Candida*, carb intake for the day should not be more than 60 to 70 grams of carbs per day at most or candida will proliferate and cravings for sugar and carbs will be abundant, but many people find they do best below 50 grams of carbs per day. Cravings for sugar and carbs are managed best by staying under 50 grams of carbs per day. People who have SIBO in addition to candida must be under 50 grams per day and may be down around 25 or lower. This means the diet is going to consist primarily of animal protein and fat. If you are just beginning to go low-carb, and are very active, have a physically demanding job, pregnant or nursing or a competitive athlete, then you may need to be on the higher end of this spectrum until your body gets better at running on fat for energy.

All meal plans and main course recipes in this cookbook will not exceed the 60 to 70 grams of carbs per day. Staying in the 60 to 70 grams of carbs per day typically allows for one small serving of fruit and nuts per day, unless one is eating a lot of high-carb vegetables like winter squash or sweet potatoes, which is not recommended. If you need to stay below 50 grams per day, then you simply do not eat the serving of fruit and nuts per day. As long as you are eating from the main course or side dish recipes provided, and keeping your servings of vegetables reasonable, you should be able to stay under 50 grams with ease. You can find charts at the end of the book to help you monitor your carb intake. Each meal should consist of a minimum of four ounces of animal protein, but possibly as much as eight ounces. Remember that a low-carb diet is not a low-calorie diet. We should eat as much animal protein and fat as needed to feel satiated.

We also learned in *Healing Chronic Candida* that there are no risks to your health by eating a low-carb diet for the long term. The human body actually prefers to run on protein and fat, it is the way we evolved, and it runs more optimally on protein and fat than it does on carbs. Carbohydrates are completely non-essential. Your body can make the minimal amount of glucose it needs through a process called gluconeogenesis, whereby it converts protein or fat into glucose. Additionally, when carbs are reduced and the body runs on fat, a byproduct of fat called ketones can be used by many cells for energy instead of glucose, including most brain cells, which decreases your need for glucose. This process is completely natural and healthy and the way our ancestors thrived for millions of years. Therefore, your body is equipped to do the same. Prior to the Agricultural revolution, our diet consisted primarily of animal protein and fat, because our ancestors simply did not have access to very many carbs. When the Agricultural revolution came along, meat and fat got replaced with carbs, and that was the beginning of decline in health in our society.

So, any fears you might have of going low-carb and consumption of animal protein and fat can be put to rest. If you need more convincing on this issue please refer back to the *Healing Chronic Candida* for more details and read the excellent work of others in the field like Mark Sisson, Nora Gedgaudas, Dr. Volek and Phinney, Dr. David Perlmutter, Dr. William Davis, Dr. Michael Eades, and Dr. Al Sears.

To refresh your memory, the paleo diet consists of foods that our ancestors ate prior to the Agricultural revolution and the basic foods permitted on the Paleo for Candida Diet include all meats, fish, eggs, and low-starch vegetables. Small servings of nuts, seeds, and low-sugar fruit may be acceptable for some. Although butter, ghee, and heavy cream are not true paleo, they are good sources of fat, which are permitted if one is not dairy intolerant and one is comfortable with not being 100 percent paleo. Occasional use of other dairy products like hard cheese, cream cheese, and full-fat yogurt may be acceptable for some as well. Most recipes in this book that include a dairy product will also offer a true paleo alternative when possible for those who wish to remain completely paleo compliant. However, dairy is kept intentionally limited in these recipes.

The diet should be completely free of sugar of any kind, including "natural" sugars like honey, maple syrup, agave, coconut sugar, etc. as well as artificial sweeteners, alcohol, caffeine, grains (including whole grains) alternative grains, legumes, and potatoes. High-carb paleo approved foods like winter squash and sweet potatoes should be reserved for special occasions. All food should be whole, unrefined, organic, grass-fed, free-range or cage-free, hormone and antibiotic free, and free of any GMOs (genetically modified organisms). Foods should be eaten in their whole and natural state as much as possible.

Designing Your Individualized Paleo for Candida Plan

Although the basics of the Paleo for Candida Diet are the same for everyone, there are many aspects of the diet that need to be individualized based on each person's unique set of circumstances and biochemistry. I call this creating your Individualized Paleo Plan (IPP), or in this case, your Individualized Paleo for "Candida" Plan. You will first need to experiment with your protein, fat, and carb ratio to find what works best for you, all of which can be affected by a wide array of factors like where you are in the healing path, other conditions you may be dealing with, activity level, age, heritage, phase of life, stress level, sex, genetics, toxin load, adrenal health, and degree of carbohydrate intolerance. Generally speaking, the plate should consist of animal protein, fat, and carb, in that order. However, depending on the aforementioned factors, this may differ somewhat in some people. If you want to be ketogenic, then it would be fat, protein, and carb in that order.

The diet will also vary based on individual food sensitivities, whether an autoimmune disorder or SIBO are present in addition to candida, and how the person responds to foods that are high in histamine, glutamate, oxalates, and FODMAPs. Therefore, your recipes and meal plans may need to be tweaked with substitutions for your own personal needs. We'll provide some additional information below on each of these aspects to help you know what to look for and I'll often make suggestions within the recipes for possible alternatives for these circumstances. However, do remember, that in most cases, we don't remove the following food groups completely, we moderate them according to our threshold for each one, as discussed in great detail in the *Healing Chronic Candida* book.

AUTOIMMUNE DISORDERS

If you have an autoimmune disorder in addition to candida, then you may want to restrict or limit the following foods, as each of them can prompt an immune response and perpetuate your condition.

- eggs
- nightshades
- nuts and seeds
- coconut
- all dairy

Get tested for food sensitivities and remove these as well.

HIGH HISTAMINE OR TYRAMINE FOODS

If you have high histamine or histamine intolerance, which commonly accompanies candida or bacterial overgrowth, then you may need to moderate the following foods, which are either high in histamine or have the ability to incite the release of histamine.

There are many other foods that are high in histamine or stimulate its release, which we have not listed here because they are already eliminated on the Paleo for Candida Diet. The foods below are the foods that you may see on a paleo diet that have that potential.

- yogurt (depending on what bacteria is present)
- sour cream
- vinegar-cured foods (e.g. mayonnaise and pickles)
- anything cured
- dried fruit
- citrus (oranges, tangerines, mandarin, lemon, lime, grapefruit, kumquat, tangelo)
- kefir, cultured or fermented vegetables, and bone broth I do not have any recipes that include kefir, cultured or fermented vegetables, and bone broth, due to the fact that most people with candida and/or SIBO have problems with these foods due to their high level of histamine and glutamate. However, their consumption is abundantly encouraged in the paleo world, so you want to be sure you are aware they have great potential for exacerbation of symptoms.
- thyme
- grapes
- aged cheese
- walnuts
- cashews
- avocados

- eggplant
- spinach
- tomatoes
- pork
- chicken liver
- chicken skin and bones (use boneless and skinless). I've also found that thighs are higher than breasts.
- beef liver
- some species of fish are more prone to histamine like mackerel, mahi-mahi, tuna, anchovies, herring, sardines, shellfish, or any fish that is stored for extended periods of time before freezing, including those in a can. However, most other forms of fish have the potential as well, depending on how it is handled and processed. The longer the fish sits out before being frozen after the catch, the higher the histamine level will be present.
- smoked fish or smoked meats.
- anything with benzoates or sulfites
- cinnamon, chili powder, cloves, anise, nutmeg, curry powder, cayenne
- anything that utilizes microbial fermentation.
- leftovers (particularly meat). The longer leftover meat sits, the more histamine will accumulate. Keep them only for a day or two. Some people can't even eat leftovers the very next day. Freezing your leftovers will prevent histamine build up.
- bananas
- pineapple
- papaya
- strawberries
- raspberries
- nuts
- egg white (when raw)
- all berries are high in benzoates and benzoates release histamine.
- pumpkin and its seeds
- olives (however, olive oil contains less, so it might be tolerated by some. Additionally, olive oil can increase the DAO enzyme, so it's not a black and white situation. You can test and see how you do.)

People who are sensitive to histamine are typically sensitive to tyramine (a byproduct of tyrosine breakdown). Many of the foods that are high in histamine are also high in tyramine like anything fermented, pickled, or cured, aged cheese, fish, aged meat, nuts and seeds, avocado, and citrus fruits. However, other foods high in tyramine include olives, yeast extracts, sweet potato, potato, and pineapple. Grilling increases amines and so can slow cooking.

Buy frozen meat whenever possible, as it is generally lower in histamine. However, if the manufacturer didn't freeze the meat immediately after processing, it may still have high histamine. You may have to try many different manufacturers to find some that is tolerable for you. Even then, there may not be consistency in the processing time. One batch might be fine and then the next batch may be too high.

When buying fresh, be sure to look at the expiration date. You want the expiration to be at least a week out. If it expires that day or the next day, then histamine is likely too high. If the meat smells even slightly sour or like ammonia, the bacteria level is high, which means high histamine. It can be very difficult to find meat that is not contaminated with bacteria, even in the organic, grass-fed arena. I throw away a lot of meat into the yard for the birds and other wildlife.

HIGH GLUTAMATE FOODS

Many of the foods that would be high in glutamate are already removed from the Paleo for Candida Diet for other reasons, so we won't mention that long list. However, if you have excess glutamate, which also commonly accompanies candida or bacterial overgrowth (discussed in great detail in *Healing Chronic Candida*), then you may need to moderate some of the following foods that are commonly used in paleo circles:

- whey protein
- milk casein (especially cheese)
- gelatin
- carageenan or vegetable gum
- guar gum
- kombu extract
- Be careful with spice blends, which commonly has MSG added or other unidentified natural flavorings that can increase glutamate.
- xanthan gum
- walnuts
- mushrooms
- broccoli
- tomatoes
- oysters
- chicken skin and chicken meat itself to a lesser extent
- meat with bone in
- cooking meat for a long time (particularly braising)
- bone broth

HIGH OXALATE FOODS

If you have elevated levels of oxalates, which also frequently occurs with candida overgrowth (and discussed in great detail in *Healing Chronic Candida*), then you may need to moderate some of the following foods:

- spinach
- beets
- swiss chard
- collards
- parsley
- cashews
- pecans
- almonds
- berries
- rhubarb
- sweet potato
- leeks
- okra
- lemon, lime, and orange peel
- black pepper
- sesame seeds
- kiwi
- figs
- tangerines
- carrots
- summer squash
- celery

Cooking your food can reduce oxalate content, but how much is eliminated depends on the method of cooking. One study found that oxalate content was reduced 30 to 87% by boiling, while steaming reduced it by 5 to 53 %. It will also help reduce phytic acid, which can inhibit absorption of minerals. I typically recommend steaming over boiling, because boiling results in loss of nutrient content, while steaming does not. However, if there is an immediate need to lower really high levels of oxalates, then boiling may be best until levels are decreased.

The following are also high in oxalates, but they should already be eliminated because they do not belong on the Paleo for Candida Diet: potatoes, chocolate/cocoa, peanuts, wheat bran and germ, tea, instant coffee, quinoa, soy protein, and tofu.

HIGH FODMAPS FOODS

If you have SIBO, IBS, or other symptoms in response to these foods (fructans, galactans, lactose, and polyols) then you may need to moderate some of the following foods:

Fructans

The popular supplement called FOS (FOS feeds candida as well), inulin, chicory, artichokes, onions, scallions/leeks, garlic, cabbage, snow peas, Brussels sprouts, shallots, watermelon, okra, pistachios, fennel, radish, broccoli, lettuce, beetroot, butternut squash, and asparagus (garlic oil and green tops of scallions are okay). Wheat, barley, and rye fall under this category, but they should already be eliminated.

Galactans

All beans like lentils, kidney beans, black-eyed peas, and garbanzos (chickpeas,) as well as broccoli and soy based products. All of which, except broccoli, should already be eliminated.

Lactose

Lactose is a naturally occurring sugar that is present in the milk of cows, goats, and sheep. Some people are deficient in an enzyme called lactase that is necessary to digest lactose properly, which results in an intolerance to food products that contain lactose, commonly called lactose intolerance. The enzyme may be completely or partially missing, which affects how severe the intolerance will be.

Lactose is most plentiful in milk, cottage cheese, soft cheese, ice cream, yogurt, and custard. Butter and cream contain only minute traces, so many people who are lactose intolerant can eat butter and cream with no problem. Ghee does not contain any lactose. However, do note that if someone who is lactose intolerant eats raw dairy, then it provides the enzymes needed to break down the lactose, so many people who are lactose intolerant have no problems with raw dairy products. The pasteurization process removes the enzymes that are present in milk that help with digestion.

Fructose

Fructose is a predominant sugar found in fruit. As we discussed previously, fruit should be minimized due to its ability to feed candida, increase blood glucose, and fuel cravings for sugar and carbs. However, if one has a problem with FODMAPs, then even small amounts of certain fruit can compound the problem. The issue at hand here is called fructose malabsorption. Some people are deficient in a fructose transporter that should be present in the small intestine called GLUT5, which results in an inability to absorb fructose completely.

However, not all fruit is subject to this issue equally. Fruit also contains glucose, and if there is a glucose/fructose ratio of 1:1 in a particular fruit, then it will have less negative impact than fruits that have more fructose than glucose. The individual with fructose malabsorption typically must be cautious with all fruit, but more so with the ones that have the higher level of fructose over glucose. Additionally, it's important to be aware that fruit that is ripe is lower in fructose than fruit that is not ripe, so fruit should always be ripe when consumed. Fruit that is not ripe is also higher in resistant starch, which feeds SIBO.

Foods that are high in fructose include the following: honey, all dried fruit, fruit juices, apples, peaches, cherries, grapes, mangoes, pears, coconut, watermelon, artichokes, eggplant, and asparagus. Sweet corn, agave, high fructose corn syrup, some wines like sherry and port, are part of this group, but should already be eliminated for obvious reasons.

Please note that fructose malabsorption is a different condition than hereditary fructose intolerance. Heredity fructose intolerance is a very serious and somewhat rare genetic disorder whereby a defective gene leads to a deficiency in an enzyme that is necessary to break down fructose, called aldolase B. In this case, all fructose must be eliminated.

Polyols

Erythritol, xylitol, mannitol, sorbitol, malitol, isomalt, and the supplement inositol. Cherries, peaches, apples, plums, nectarines, apricots, pears, blackberries, persimmons, watermelon, prunes, avocado, celery, cauliflower, green bell pepper, button mushrooms, snow peas, and sweet potato.

SIBO IN ADDITION TO CANDIDA

If you have SIBO in addition to candida, then you should be aware that your carb intake may need to be even lower. Perhaps not more than 25 or 30 grams per day or less. Many people do best going close to zero. SIBO also feeds on fiber and resistant starch in addition to the carbs. Additionally, symptoms can be significantly lowered by cooking your vegetables, fruit, and nuts until they are soft. This reduces fiber and resistant starch levels, providing less fuel for SIBO. All foods in the FODMAPs category will need to be moderated as well, and people with SIBO tend to have elevated levels of glutamate and histamine, so these foods will most likely need to be moderated.

NIGHTSHADE FAMILY

Nightshades contain a variety of substances known as lectins, alkaloids, and saponins, which can be difficult for some people to eliminate effectively and may lead to a variety of undesirable symptoms like inflammation, joint and muscle pain, abdominal pain, muscle tremors, heartburn or other digestive disturbances, and fatigue.

Alkaloids and saponins can be toxic even to a healthy individual in excess, but the person with a liver that is overwhelmed with candida toxins and impairment of the gut, is even more vulnerable. In either case, nightshades are a food group that should be moderated.

The foods in this category include ashwaganda, potato, cayenne, tomatoes, eggplant, chili peppers, habeneros, red pepper, jalapeño, bell peppers (also known as sweet peppers), paprika, tomatillos, tomarillos, pimentos, goji berries, garden huckleberries (but not regular huckleberries), cape gooseberries (but not normal gooseberries), ground cherries (but not Rainier or Bing cherries).

Most store-bought tomato products are preserved with a form of citric acid that is procured from yeast, which can kill friendly gut flora and may increase glutamate. Consumption from these sources should be minimized. Both tomatoes and eggplants have a small amount of naturally occurring nicotine, which has the ability to generate cravings for cigarettes for someone who is in the process of trying to quit, and this could have a domino effect for cravings of other substances like sugar, carbs, alcohol, or drugs.

OVERWEIGHT

If you are trying to lose weight, then you will most likely want to stay under 50 grams of carbs per day, especially if you are a postmenopausal woman. This helps the body transition from a sugar burner to a fat burner more easily. Many postmenopausal women will not lose the weight, unless they stay under 50 grams per day. If you aren't postmenopausal, weight loss will occur much faster under 50 grams per day.

UNDERWEIGHT

This is discussed in detail in the *Healing Chronic Candida* book, however, to summarize those points and refresh your memory, you'll want to increase calorie intake. Eat as much animal protein and fat as needed to feel satiated. A low-carb diet should not be low-calorie. Eat more paleo friendly carbs (chestnuts, sweet potatoes, yams, winter squash, fruit, nuts, and seeds) if you can do so without a significant increase in symptoms. Be sure to add liberal quantities of fat to these foods in the form of butter, ghee, or oil.

Increase your serving sizes of meat and fat in each meal, eat fattier cuts of meat, increase high-calorie foods such as coconut oil, olive oil, avocado oil, butter, ghee, heavy cream, olives, and avocados as often as possible. Add liberal amounts of butter, ghee, or permitted oils to your vegetables and meat. Eat shortly before going to bed so you don't have time to burn it off.

INDIVIDUAL FACTORS

How you respond to a particular food will also affect whether it should be included in your diet plan as well. Any food, regardless of its category, that produces symptoms or cravings, is subject to moderation or elimination. However, the severity of those symptoms may be a deciding factor, whereby a food that produces severe or unbearable symptoms or cravings should be eliminated completely, but a food that generates only a few minor symptoms may be moderated. Sometimes it may be a matter of quantity, a small serving may produce no symptoms, but a larger serving does.

FOOD SENSITIVITIES

If you have sensitivities to a particular food that is generally permitted on the diet, it should be removed as well. Consumption of these foods will contribute to inflammation in the gut, which will then promote more overgrowth of candida or other pathogens. Additionally, cravings for the offending food typically occur in the advanced stage of sensitivity, and these cravings can then snowball into cravings for sugar and carbs. Not only that, some people experience a psychotropic affect from the offending foods, which can lead to uncontrollable cravings for sugar and carbs and compulsive overeating.

Paleo for Candida
Breakfast Ideas

Deciding what to have for breakfast and letting go of long-held beliefs and conditioning about what types of food should be included in a breakfast meal is the most difficult aspect of the diet for nearly everyone when they first get started. One of the questions I am asked most often by my clients and website visitors is "what should I have for breakfast?" Contrary to popular belief, breakfast should not consist of cereal, toast, waffles, muffins, bagels, or pancakes, or even what some consider to be more healthy, like whole grains, fruit and nuts, smoothies, potatoes, alternative grain products, granola, buckwheat pancakes, or any other high-carb food.

Not only is breakfast the most important meal of the day, what you put in that breakfast is even more important. A breakfast that is heavy, or even moderate, in carbs not only feeds candida and other microbes, which incites a cascade of associated symptoms, but it also sets you up for the day for mood swings, low energy, mid-morning hunger, an increase in appetite and cravings for sugar and carbs, brain fog and poor cognitive function, and weight gain. Starting your day with a breakfast that is rich in animal protein and fat and low in carbs will alleviate candida and other microbial related symptoms, supply you with energy throughout the morning, encourage a more stable mood and lower anxiety levels, prevent brain fog and improve cognitive activity, curb mid-morning hunger and cravings for sugar and carbs, and switch on your fat burning metabolism.[1]

Our Paleolithic ancestors (and even our grandparents) flourished on animal protein for breakfast, which more often than not, was obtained from the hunt and prey acquired the night before and this is what we thrive most optimally on as well. Therefore, the recipes in the main course meal section of this book are what should be used for breakfast and they can be accompanied by the side dishes as needed. Your breakfast plate should resemble your lunch and dinner plate—meaning it will consist of animal protein, fat, and low-starch vegetables.

Although we don't typically have a carcass lying around to munch on in the morning as our ancestors did, we do have leftovers in the fridge from our dinner the night before, which makes a perfect, quick, easy, and nutrient packed breakfast. In order to save time and reduce stress in a busy morning, ensuring that you cook enough dinner so that there will be plenty left over for breakfast is a practice you will want to adopt on a regular basis. Alternatively, if you want to prepare a fresh breakfast, that is just as good. Here are some ideas to get you started either way:

- Meat loaf and steamed vegetables.

- Stew.

- Baked chicken breast and steamed vegetables.

- Steak, eggs, and stir-fry cabbage.

- Roast beef and steamed vegetables.

- Buffalo burger wrapped in lettuce and topped with avocado.

- Lamb chops and steamed vegetables.

- Baked salmon and scrambled eggs with spinach.

- Hard boiled eggs and avocado.

- Crustless quiche.

- Nitrate-free and sugar-free sausage with vegetable of choice.

- Any of the main course meals in this book would be a great option.

- If your metabolism and level of overgrowth allow, a small piece of fruit may accompany your animal protein and vegetables at breakfast from time to time, but it should never take their place.

- Coffee, green tea, hot chocolate, or any beverage that contains caffeine should be avoided, because they all disrupt brain chemistry and the endocrine system, which will lead to cravings for sugar and carbs, fuel sympathetic dominance, and degrade gut health. Try to get away from the habit of a warm beverage in the morning and drink a glass of water instead. Alternatively, you can replace the coffee, tea, or hot chocolate with a cup of herbal tea. Remember, that decaf is not free of caffeine, it only contains a lesser amount, which should not be consumed either.

Although you may feel uncomfortable about eating these types of food for breakfast at first, it is only because you are changing a learned behavior. In a short amount of time, it will seem like the natural and normal choice and you'll no longer think about those unhealthy high-carb breakfasts. The improvement in symptoms will also be a great motivator.

Tips for Staying on Track

Getting started on the Paleo for Candida Diet and remaining compliant is often one of the most difficult challenges for people to overcome in the beginning. Cravings for sugar, carbs, caffeine, chocolate, grains, etc. can be overwhelming and sabotage even the best of efforts. The primary key to remember is that cravings for these foods are eliminated by removing them from your diet. I know this may seem counterintuitive, as most people think they must eliminate their cravings in order to stop eating these foods. But, the reality is that the cravings will not disappear as long as you continue to eat them.

It is the consumption of these foods that fuels the addiction process to them. Sugar, caffeine, chocolate, grains, and foods that are high in carbs (including complex carbs like whole grains, potatoes, legumes and even too much fruit), disrupt the endocrine system and neurotransmitters in the brain, which leads to cravings for more sugar, carbs, caffeine, etc. When you remove these foods from the diet and replace them with animal protein and fat (which is what the human body prefers to run on and runs most optimally with), it will allow your brain and endocrine system to normalize, at which time your cravings begin to dissipate. The less sugar, carbs, grains, caffeine, etc. that you eat the less you will want them. Therefore, it is consistency with the diet that leads to success.

This will require that you have a sincere desire to change and a strong commitment to yourself and your healing journey. At first, it will take a lot of concerted effort to (gently, but firmly) push yourself to do what is required. You may not be completely onboard with some aspects of your plan and you may face a lot of inner resistance, both physically and emotionally. You will be doing some things you don't want to do and it may feel unnatural for a while.

However, once you begin to understand how sugar and carbs affect your mind and body and as you start to experience a reduction in symptoms and improvement in health from the changes you make in diet, it will help you develop more inner strength, determination, self-discipline, motivation, a strong conviction, and strengthen your commitment, all of which creates a positive feedback loop that makes remaining on the diet easier and eventually desirable. Once your body makes the transition from running on carbs to running on protein and fat, you will no longer think about or want the sugar, carbs, etc. and you will grow to appreciate your new way of eating. Eventually, you'll be drawn towards protein and fat instead of carbs. The initial part of this process, which is the most difficult, takes about two to three weeks in most people, but may take up to six weeks for some.[2] Use the following tips to help support yourself through this process.

FIRST INGREDIENT (MINDSET)

The first ingredient that the Paleo for Candida Diet demands from everyone is a new mindset and approach to eating. We have all been molded by our family, media, health care providers, and society to believe certain things about our diet, food choices, and food related behaviors and events, many of which are based on myths, lies, addiction, or misinformation that lead to degradation of mental and physical health. The way you've been taught to eat, your relationship with food, and its place in your life do not support health.

In order to remain compliant with your diet, you will have to wipe the plate clean by letting go of preconceived beliefs and attitudes and social conditioning about the way a meal should look, taste, or be prepared, and the relationship you have with food. You will need to redefine not only your meal planning, recipes, and interactions, but most likely your identity in relation to food as well. Although food can be part of a joyous occasion, our happiness or quality of food related experiences should not be found in the consumption of sugar and carbs. Our joy in life should be found in our connection with self, others, and the Universe or whatever spiritual deity you identify with.

You must be willing to go against the grain, resist the pressure to fit in with the crowd, and stand proud of the fact that you are taking the road less traveled.

GET THEM OUT OF THE HOUSE

Once you've made the decision to make these changes in your diet, get the sugar, caffeine, chocolate, grains, legumes, alcohol, and high-carb foods (or any other food that is a trigger for you) out of the house, so you will not be tempted to give in during times of hunger, stress, habit, or a weak moment. An individual who is trying to overcome alcohol or drug addiction would not bring alcohol or drugs into the household, the same principle applies here. You are breaking an addiction that can be just as powerful. It will be extremely difficult to be successful if you are surrounded by these foods. It should be a rule that these types of foods are not permitted in the household. Make a list of the new foods you'll be eating and stock up. Additionally, changes in diet are more successful when it is a family event.

Do not feel guilty about how this may affect others in the family. If there are children in the household, they should be following the new diet as well. There is a strong likelihood that if you have a problem with candida overgrowth, so do your children. Yeast overgrowth is rampant in children in our society, due to a diet high in sugar and carbs and the overuse of antibiotics. Even if they don't, permitting them to eat sugar, grains, high-carbs, caffeine, and chocolate sets them up for conditions like attention deficit, hyperactivity, and behavioral problems as a child, and depression, anxiety disorders, insulin resistance, type 2 diabetes, obesity, cancer, heart disease, eating disorders, addiction, and Alzheimer's later in life. You are not depriving them of anything by restricting these foods. Teaching your children to eat by the basic principles found in the Paleo for Candida Diet is one of the most loving and responsible actions you can take as a parent.

Spouses and partners can be more of a challenge since you have no control over their choices and they may be resistant to change. Ideally, they should make changes in their diet as well, but at the very least, they should support you in your goals and be willing not to bring these substances into the house. Many people who struggle with sugar and carb addiction have a history of highly dysfunctional or abusive relationships, which puts them in a state of chronic stress that can provide constant fuel for cravings for sugar, carbs, caffeine, etc. If your partner actively berates you, discourages, or sabotages you, then you need to consider whether this is a relationship that is in your best interest. It is your health and life that is at stake. The type of person you would choose for a life partner can change significantly once you correct brain chemistry and disruption in the endocrine system.

BUILD A SUPPORT SYSTEM

Changing the way you think about diet, food, meal planning, etc. requires that you reinforce the new principles, habits, and goals you are trying to adopt, and reinforcement is achieved with constancy and repetition. If everyone in your life is eating sugar, carbs, caffeine, etc., and encouraging you to do so, questioning your new path, or planting doubts in your head, it's going to be quite difficult to remain compliant and committed to the changes you are trying to make.

You need at least one person, but preferably more, to help you break free from conditioning, reprogram, and strengthen your new mindset. Try and bring other people into your life who are health oriented and have at least some nutritional awareness who can support you on your new path, or at least don't sabotage you. Ideally, they will be paleo enthusiasts or at least low-carb lovers.

A health coach, nutritionist, psychotherapist, or counselor can be a great asset as well, to provide encouragement, keep things in perspective, help you cope and adjust, clarify goals, and stay on track. If you can find a buddy who is transitioning to the Paleo for Candida Diet, they can provide the same, plus you could call one another when you have a weak moment, remind one another why you are doing what you are doing and how horrible you will feel if you indulge. You could have an agreement in place whereby you plan ahead what you will say to one another to have the most powerful impact.

Visit websites, forums, online communities, or groups and meet-ups in your hometown if possible who share similar values and beliefs. Don't put yourself in situations where temptation will be nearly impossible to resist. Avoid socializing at bakeries, cookie factories, pizza shops, and coffee houses, in the same way that an alcoholic would not hang out in the bar. Once you get stronger in your conviction and your brain chemistry and endocrine system begin to repair, then these places will not be such a temptation, but in the beginning they should be avoided; the more avenues in your life that reinforce your new principles, the better.

Reading books that are promoting the principles you are adopting can be a powerful reinforcer. Some great books that everyone should read who is getting started on this path include *The Primal Blueprint* by Mark Sisson, *The Art and Science of Low-Carbohydrate Living* by Dr. Stephen Phinney and Jeff Volek, *Primal Body Primal Mind* by Nora

Gedgaudas, *The Paleo Diet* by Loren Cordain, *Grain Brain* by Dr. David Perlmutter, *Wheat Belly* by Dr. William Davis, *End Your Addiction Now* by Dr. C.E. Gant, and *Keto Clarity* by Jimmy Moore. Also, take a look at the work of Dr. Michael Eades, and Dr. Al Sears.

On the other hand, finding people in your own community who are living and eating by the same principles you will be following are few and far between. Even many health conscious people will still be consuming a lot of substances that are off limits for you, like coffee, chocolate, and high-carb foods. So, support is usually limited. This cannot be used as an excuse for non-compliance, lack of commitment, etc. You must be a maverick and develop the ability to stand strong on your own two feet in the presence of sugar, caffeine, carbs, grains, etc. and be proud of your choices and the path that you are following.

PREPARE FOR SOME DOWN TIME

Initially, giving up sugar, carbs, caffeine, chocolate, etc., can be just as difficult as overcoming an addiction to alcohol and drugs. There will be significant discomfort and withdrawal for a week or two. Your ability to perform daily activities may be temporarily impaired. Before beginning the diet, make preparations ahead of time that allow you to devote some time to this transition period. Recruit friends and family members to help out with childcare, running errands, household tasks, cooking meals, etc. Clear your schedule, reduce distractions, and minimize unnecessary stress as much as possible. If you work outside the home, then this is the perfect time to use up some of your vacation time. Try and get at least one week, but preferably two weeks, free to focus on yourself and achieve this goal.

INFORM OTHERS

Make sure other people in your life (loved ones, spouses, significant others, children, family members, co-workers, neighbors, friends, etc.) know about your changes in diet. Tell them what you do and do not eat and what you are trying to accomplish. Ask them not to give you sugar, chocolate, caffeine, etc. as a gift at holidays, birthdays, etc. and to support you in your process. This will help you be more accountable. You'll be less likely to give in to temptation in their presence, since they would then know that you are breaking your commitment.

PLAN AHEAD

Your new way of eating is going to take more time and preparation, so you'll need to plan ahead to reduce stress, ensure that good food choices are available at all times, and avoid sabotaging yourself. The easier you can make this on yourself, the less disruptive it will be and the smoother the transition. After you've been at it for a while, you'll adjust and find your own ways of fitting things into your schedule with more ease. It will become just another part of your day-to-day regimen. Additionally, as you begin to feel better and cravings begin to wane, you'll feel more motivated to invest the time and energy that is needed for meal planning.

One of the best ways to cut down on preparation time is to cook in batches instead of individual meals. Then you can serve the food in a variety of different ways throughout the day. For example, a batch of chicken breasts can be served hot and coated with butter and garlic for supper, then the next day at breakfast could be cut into cubes and tossed in a salad, and at lunch could be added to some soup. An extra large meat loaf can last the whole day. The same tip can be applied to vegetables. Steam vegetables for the entire day and then serve them in a variety of different ways at each meal (e.g. sautéed, chopped, pureed into soup). I have demonstrated how to put this into action in the sample meal plans further ahead.

Always cook extra meat so that you can keep some in the freezer for emergencies, snacks, or a quick lunch. For example, in my own life, I cook enough meat and vegetables each morning for that day, so that all I have to do is heat up my lunch and dinner. I often cook enough for the following day as well and I always have a half meat loaf, a couple chicken breasts, or several burgers, etc. in the freezer, that only need to be thawed to be ready to eat. Alternatively, you may prefer to cook everything for the next day the night before, if your mornings are too busy. Be sure to make something that you can take to work with you for lunch.

Another option is the crock pot. You can toss all your ingredients in a crock pot to cook overnight so it's ready the next morning. Put enough in there for breakfast, lunch and dinner or put it on in the morning before you go to work so it's ready for supper and then use the leftovers for breakfast and lunch the next day. However, do be aware, that slow cooking can increase glutamate levels. So, if you have elevated glutamate, this may not be an acceptable option for you.

Think ahead about situations that may set you up to fall and have a plan in place. For example, if you know you won't be home in time for lunch when you have to go out run errands, then pack a lunch and stick it in a little cooler in the car. If you're in a hurry, pull one of those frozen burgers you should have in the freezer and bring it with you to hold you over until you get home. There are too many unhealthy options at your fingertips, if you allow hunger to set in before getting home, you may simply say "the heck with it" and then pay the price later.

If you're going to a social or business event that involves food and beverage, you can eat at home before going, and then sip on sparkling mineral water at the function. Alternatively, find out ahead of time what is on the menu and be sure there is something less offensive you can choose, like steak and a salad, and skip the dessert. Know in advance what you will order, so you won't get caught off guard and try to fit in with the crowd. You could also bring your own food with you and put it on a plate to make it look as if were acquired from the event. Remember, do not be ashamed to stand up for healthy eating.

KEEP IT SIMPLE

If you've spent time on my blog, then you may have heard me say, I am no Martha Stewart. If it's not quick and easy, it's not going to happen for me. Additionally, eating in a manner that supports health in people with candida, SIBO, sugar addiction, adrenal fatigue and other related conditions is about returning to the fundamentals. Furthermore, even healthy paleo approved foods can encourage overgrowth of candida and other microbes, elicit cravings for sugar and carbs, and foster poor health if they are processed or combined in a certain way (e.g. cakes, cookies, pastries, and other baked goods).

Although it is acceptable to have something like this once in a blue moon, they should not be consumed on a daily basis. Therefore, the recipes you will find in this book are not elegant or designed to impress. Many people, especially those who love to cook, get hung up on trying to create meals that look like they came from a five star restaurant. Let go of the need to design a masterpiece and stick with the basics.

STAY FOCUSED

One of the biggest mistakes people make when trying to make changes in their diet is that they listen to too many voices at one time. As you likely know, there are hundreds of dietary approaches out there to choose from and every healthcare practitioner may follow a different one. If you try to follow dietary advice of too many people at the same time, you end up lost, confused, and stuck. You must shut out all the noise and stay focused on one dietary path at a time. In order for this diet to work its magic, you must be 100 percent committed to this path and this path only.

MAKE YOUR DIET THE #1 PRIORITY

Eating the proper diet should be at the very top of your priority list. No excuses are acceptable. It is not negotiable. Without the proper diet in place, nothing else you do along the healing journey is likely to be effective or long-lasting. You must be willing to invest the time, energy, and additional effort that is required if you want to reap the benefits.

Almost everything in our fast-paced modern world is destructive to health. You must create a life that fosters good health. That means you will have to change who you hang out with, where you hang out, activities you engage in, how you interact with the world, etc. If the manner in which you live does not enable you to make the changes in diet that are necessary to improve health, then the manner in which you live must change.

BECOME PASSIONATE ABOUT YOUR DIET

Get passionate about diet, nutrition, experimenting in the kitchen, paleo principles, learning everything you can about your body and how to individualize the diet for your unique biochemical needs, and the healing journey. Instead of focusing on how hard it is, focus on what you can do to achieve the goal. When you become passionate about your diet (or anything else), you become unstoppable. No challenge, road block, social pressure, craving, etc. will be big enough to break your commitment.

YOU'VE BEEN GIVEN A GIFT

Do not allow yourself to look at this situation as if you are being deprived or forbidden to indulge in delicious treats. Reframe the way you think about the sugar, carbs, grains, caffeine, legumes, chocolate, etc., refer to them as toxins, drugs, and poisons, that are destructive to your mental and physical health, because that is the reality of the circumstance. You haven't really lost anything, except a bunch of substances that cause insulin resistance, type 2 diabetes, obesity, heart disease, cancer, Alzheimer's, addiction, and more. You are better off in the long run without them.

What you have learned about diet is an incredible gift that can help you reach a higher level of health, improve the quality of your life, and maybe even increase your life expectancy. Keep focused on these positive aspects, rather than what you have to give up. Don't say you "can't" eat sugar, grains, caffeine, etc. Say I "don't" eat sugar, high-carb foods etc. Saying you "can't" implies you are being forced to do something. Saying you "don't" implies you have a made a choice, which is empowering. Be grateful and appreciative for the knowledge you have acquired and the new path you are following.

However, if you do feel deprived, you are at greater risk for cheating and self-destructive behavior like binging. Use the recipes in the dessert section of this book as substitutions for some of the foods that are now restricted, if these feelings arise. But, do remain reasonable and don't eat anything that causes a notable increase in symptoms or puts you out of commission. As you begin to heal and cravings subside, then feelings of deprivation will eventually dissipate.

MINDFUL EATING

When you are more mindful of your food and your eating experience, it enhances communication and signaling from neurotransmitters and hormones, which will subdue cravings for sugar and carbs, control appetite, and ward off overeating. Meals taste better and richer and are more satiating and the act of eating is a more satisfying experience. It also improves digestion, which enhances your ability to absorb nutrients that will support the immune system, brain function, gut health, etc., fosters a more positive mood and more inner peace, heightens feelings of well-being, and facilitates a deeper connection with your spiritual source.

To cultivate mindfulness in this area, begin by eliminating distractions. Put your cell phone in a different room or turn it off. Separate yourself from the laptop, computer, tablet, mail, books, television, and magazines. Engage in no other activities during meal time. Sit at a table while eating. This forces you to focus on your food and what you are doing. Slow down and be fully present with your meals and the activity of eating.

Don't scarf your food down mindlessly. Sit "with" your food and bask in the eating experience. Be completely present with nothing but the moment and what is taking place with your food. Focus on and recognize the full worth of each food's unique qualities: its shape, color, texture, aroma, temperature, nutrient content, how it sounds and feels against your lips and in your mouth. Chew slowly and intentionally. Be conscious of and engaged with each bite and sensation, as if nothing else in the world exists in that moment.

When the food is in your mouth, close your eyes periodically and relish in the food and the entire experience of eating. Fully appreciate each bite and all the characteristics of your food and sensations that take place. Savor each moment and morsel. Be with your meal and the experience of eating as if they are the focal point of a meditation or you are engaged in a tender lovemaking session with the love of your life for the first time.

Don't jump up as soon as you're finished, sit back for a moment and reflect on what you just experienced before moving on to your next activity, like how exquisite the food tasted, the sensations, and how it looked and smelled. Integrate the experience into your being. You may also want to acknowledge gratitude internally, or to your spiritual source, for the food and the experience.

Additionally, when you eat too quickly, your brain doesn't get the message from your gut that it doesn't need anymore until it's too late and you've already eaten too much. Slowing it down will get that message to the brain sooner, which turns off appetite and cravings and allows you to feel satiated.

Apart from the actual act of eating, the principles of mindfulness should be extended to all aspects surrounding your meal, including making good choices about the food you put in your body (e.g. organic, grass-fed, pastured, cage-free, hormone- and antibiotic-free, low-carb, no sugar, paleo), and preparation (e.g. shopping, cutting, tossing, cooking).

Being mindful of how your body responds to your meals (e.g. makes you tired, itchy, or achy, or enhances energy) can be used as a guide to make modifications and individualize your diet according to your unique biochemical needs.

It's simple, practical, and costs you absolutely nothing. Eating mindfully should be a basic principle built into your lifestyle when designing your individualized paleo plan, which is discussed in more detail on page 5. I suspect our caveman ancestors were just naturally conscious during meal time as they didn't have all the distractions and stressors to contend with that accompanies modern day life.

Furthermore, mindfulness should be practiced in all areas of your life, not just eating and meal time, to enhance health and well-being more fully.

KEEP IT GREEN

One of the most commonly overlooked and powerful triggers that can completely sabotage your ability to remain compliant on the diet is exposure to common toxins. Toxins of all kinds can disrupt brain chemistry and the endocrine system and increase sympathetic nervous system activity, all of which can result in profound cravings for sugar and carbs, binging, or an increase in appetite, as well as a wide array of neurological symptoms like anxiety, depression, headaches, impaired cognitive functioning, nervousness, weakness, trembling, attention deficit, and more.

This includes chemicals that are found in your daily life like pesticides, herbicides, air fresheners, cleaning supplies, laundry soap, dish soap, shampoo, body soap, cosmetics, perfume and cologne, as well as car exhaust, cigarette smoke, gas or propane heat, gas or propane stove or hot water tank, and mold. These items should be eliminated from the home and yard and replaced with green, non-toxic, and natural living alternatives.

MANAGE YOUR EMOTIONAL STRESS

Emotional stress can trigger compelling and uncontrollable cravings for sugar, carbs, grains, caffeine, chocolate, alcohol, etc., because it too disrupts brain chemistry and blood sugar levels and incites sympathetic nervous system activity and burdens the adrenal glands. Furthermore, our ability to control our impulses, think before acting, and put any stress management skills we may hold into action is inhibited when we are under stress. Therefore, keeping unnecessary stress to a minimum and managing stress that can't be avoided is essential.

Many people have unconsciously learned to manage their stress with the consumption of sugar, carbs, caffeine, etc. because each of these substances has the ability to temporarily increase neurotransmitters that will alleviate their stress. However, regular consumption of these substances then contributes further to disruption of brain chemistry and endocrine function, which creates a vicious cycle, whereby more of the substance is needed and a higher level of stress is generated.

Like anything that is learned, this behavior can be unlearned with the regular use of stress management techniques. My four favorite practices are deep breathing exercises, mindfulness meditation, communing with nature, and smiling frequently. You can find more in depth information on these topics in the *Healing Chronic Candida* book or on my website.

Mindfulness based meditation has been shown to be an effective adjunctive therapy in the treatment of addictions of all kinds, which means it will work well for sugar, carb, and caffeine addiction as well. It decreases anxiety, depression, stress, relapse, and cravings. People who practice mindfulness also experience greater inner peace, self-awareness, feelings of well-being, empathy, compassion, creativity, and intuition. Other good practices include things like, tai chi, yoga, Qigong, walking, art, spending time with your pet, music, community service, art, photography, and dance.

NURTURE SPIRITUAL HEALTH

On one hand, it can be very difficult to experience inner peace or a higher level of awareness or consciousness, live a life with deep meaning, purpose and authenticity that are in line with your true inner desires, and feel connected to yourself, others, the Universe, your higher purpose, or whatever spiritual beliefs you identify with and value, when brain chemistry and endocrine function are disrupted from a poor diet, environmental toxins, or overgrowth of candida and other microbes. Yet, on the other hand, lack of inner peace or serenity, connectedness, depth, meaning, authenticity, and purpose in your life, can be a significant driving force for cravings for sugar, carbs, caffeine, chocolate, etc., and to take comfort in food to fill the void.

When you are eating the proper diet and living a lifestyle that supports health and reduces overgrowth of candida and other microbes, it will enable you to become more spiritually connected and fulfilled by restoring balance to your brain chemistry and endocrine system. However, it is equally important to engage in practices that feed you spiritually (e.g. meditation, prayer, yoga, visualization, deep breathing, tai chi, Qigong, time with nature, dance, art, singing, making love, relationships with self, others and pets, community service, a hobby or whatever spiritual activities nourish you) on a regular basis to help prevent cravings and avoid turning to food that can sabotage the healing journey.

CRAVINGS ONLY LAST A FEW MINUTES

Most cravings will pass within a few minutes. When they arise, find a way to distract yourself until they are gone. Sip slowly on a glass of water, chew on a toothpick, go for a walk, pet the dog, look at the moon, sun or stars, listen to a song, meditate, do deep breathing exercises, call a friend, read something, watch TV, or do some squats. Just give your brain something else to latch onto for those few minutes and they will subside.

Although you feel compelled to fulfill a craving, simply learning that you don't have to act on them and the world will not come to an end if you don't, will empower you to say no with more comfort the next time. If you need to eat something, eat animal protein and fat. When you eat the food you are craving, this only strengthens its grip on you and reinforces more cravings. What the body really needs when you are having a sugar or carb craving is animal protein and fat; this is what will provide satiation.

However, if you must absolutely have something sweet, then use the recipes in the dessert section of this book, as they are rich in protein and fat. When a carb is accompanied by a substantial amount of fat, it lowers its glycemic index, which decreases the impact on blood sugar, insulin, and neurotransmitters. It also makes the sugars a little less potent for the microbes, resulting in less symptoms.

Additionally, thirst can be experienced as hunger or cravings, so drink a big glass of water in case that is the inciting factor.

AVOID FOOD PORN

Food porn (enticing images of food) triggers dopamine and lights up the reward center in the brain in the same way as drugs and alcohol. This incites a biological urge to seek out those foods and consume them. Studies have also shown that looking at food porn increases the release of ghrelin, our hormone that activates hunger and inactivates the area of our brain that governs self-control.[1] That means websites, magazines, commercials, cookbooks, etc. that display seductive images of foods you are trying to give up should be avoided or restricted.

DON'T SKIP MEALS

When you miss a meal, blood sugar levels drop out, which means the brain is going to send out a message that you need some glucose quickly and you'll have cravings for sugar and carbs or ravenous hunger. When blood sugar levels decline, so do neurotransmitter levels, which also prompts cravings for sugar and carbs. Prevent this from happening by keeping blood sugar stable at all times with adequate consumption of animal protein and fat throughout the day. Consumption of carbs will cause an elevation in blood sugar and then a crash. Animal protein and fat keep blood sugar at an even keel.

Eat three meals per day, no more than five hours apart, and each meal should have a minimum of four ounces of animal protein (or as much as eight ounces) that is not too lean. If you experience symptoms of low blood sugar before five hours is up, (trembling, irritability, headache, ravenous hunger, feeling weak, lightheaded, anxiety, etc.) then eat a snack that consists of animal protein and fat in between meals. If you wake up in the middle of the night with low blood sugar symptoms, then eat animal protein and fat shortly before going to bed.

AVOID INTERMITTENT FASTING

Although intermittent fasting is commonly practiced in the paleo community, please be aware that it is not right for everyone. This is especially true for the individual with candida, SIBO and the associated conditions of adrenal fatigue, impaired blood sugar regulation, sympathetic nervous system dominance, sugar and carb addiction, or anyone in the process of trying to replenish neurotransmitter levels associated with anxiety, depression, addiction, insomnia, eating disorders, or other mental health or cognitive conditions.

While it is true that intermittent fasting was a natural part of our caveman ancestor's life, our ancestors weren't living with microbial overgrowth, adrenal fatigue, disrupted brain chemistry, and impairment of the endocrine system, as much of society is today. The adrenal glands must be strong to handle the hormonal and metabolic changes that take place during intermittent fasting and the brain must not be depleted in neurotransmitters. Otherwise, intermittent fasting can magnify the aforementioned issues and precipitate even more deterioration in health.

DON'T STUFF FEELINGS AND RESOLVE CONFLICT

Unresolved conflict or suppressed emotions may lead to unconscious eating, binging, and cravings for sugar and carbs in an attempt to self-medicate. Additionally, not expressing yourself can lower self-esteem and self-worth, which makes you more vulnerable to cravings. Communicate honestly and openly in your relationships and deal with conflict directly.

BE PHYSICALLY ACTIVE

Regular physical activity improves leptin and insulin sensitivity, which means less problems with blood sugar fluctuations and a decrease in appetite and cravings. It also stimulates neurotransmitter activity, which will modulate mood, appetite, and cravings, enhances the immune and detoxification systems and motility. However, too much exercise is just as bad as not enough. Exercising for too long or too hard can overstimulate neurotransmitters and contribute to depletion, produces excess sympathetic nervous system activity, lower immunity, and disrupt blood glucose levels, which then leads to an increase in cravings for sugar and carbs and more microbial overgrowth. Walking, yoga, tai chi and other low-impact exercise combined with occasional bursts of high-impact activity provides a good balance. Studies show that remaining physically active throughout your day is much more important and health enhancing than a structured exercise routine at the gym, so just keep moving. We should move slowly, but frequently; and occasionally we should lift heavy things and sprint.[2]

GET ADEQUATE SLEEP

Lack of sleep causes neurotransmitters and hormones that regulate appetite and blood sugar levels to be less responsive leading to an increase in cravings, increases sympathetic nervous system activity, and lowers immune function. Sleep is also vital for regulating gut motility and the migrating motor complex, which play a significant role in the health of your gut. Insufficient sleep causes an elevation in ghrelin (our hunger hormone) and a decrease in leptin (our satiation hormone). Sleep deficit also triggers regions of the brain that drive us to seek out rewards in the form of quick fixes like sugar, carbs, and other junk food, and inhibits regions of the brain associated with executive function, which enable us to resist our cravings and make better choices. It is critical that you make sleep a priority in your life. If you don't get enough sleep through the night, take naps during the day.

COMMUNE WITH NATURE AND THE SUN

Spending time with nature and getting adequate sunlight has been shown to boost neurotransmitter levels, which lowers our sympathetic nervous system activity and consequently our stress levels, boosts mood, moderates appetite, and enhances immune function. It also increases overall feelings of well-being, inner peace, and transcendental connectedness. All of which can help reduce cravings for sugar and carbs and/or increase your ability to resist temptations that may arise.

BEFRIEND YOUR INNER SABOTEUR

Anytime you try to make changes in your life, there are likely to be inner voices that will object, rebel, or resist. They may tell you this is the wrong path, this is too scary, it's too hard, it's too expensive, it's too weird, don't listen to her she's crazy, blah, blah, blah. The list of protests can be endless. These voices are the result of conditioning from our parents, siblings, teachers, friends, significant others, health care system, government, and society. Recognize them for what they are, reassure them that you are on the right track, and move forward anyhow. Push past the fear and objections. Once they see that you are right, which will be demonstrated by the reduction in symptoms and improvement in health, they will quiet down and then they will actually begin to work for you instead of against you. Eventually, the voices will begin to object and resist if you stray from the Paleo for Candida Diet and encourage you to remain committed.

REMEMBER THE TRUE MEANING OF HOLIDAYS

Sadly, nearly all of our holidays are traditionally associated with the consumption of alcohol, sugar, chocolate, caffeine, and/or lots of high-carbs foods, all of which can be very difficult for many people to resist, especially in the early phases of transitioning to a healthier diet. The first and most important step to prevent the holidays from sabotaging your diet and impeding your healing journey is to remember that the true meaning of any holiday is about spending time with the people you love, not the sugar, alcohol, and chocolate.

Change the way you think about celebrations by creating new holiday traditions that are focused more on your relationships, rather than what you are eating or drinking. Play board games, take walks or go hiking, watch movies, make arts and crafts, visit a museum or engage in any other enjoyable activity that connects you with the significant people in your life. Your holidays can be just as memorable, fun, and joyous without the presence of sugar, chocolate, alcohol, etc.

Again, don't feel guilty for regulating these substances from children that may be present in the home. Your household should remain free of sugar, chocolate, alcohol, carbs, etc, even on the holidays. This will teach your children to value the experience of the holiday more than the food, help them build healthier expectations and the ability to exercise self-control.

However, as you will see in the recipes in this book, a birthday cake can be made without sugar and wheat, candy like treats can be made with coconut, fudge can be made from carob and nut butter, cookies can be free of grains and sugar, apple pie is just as classic without wheat and sugar, and egg nog is delicious without sugar and alcohol. So, you do not have to go without on the holidays, you just have to learn to create healthier alternatives.

Halloween

Even with all the ghosts, witches, and goblins floating around, the most frightening aspect of Halloween is the poison (sugar) the children will bring home and put into their bodies. What? Poison, you say. Yes, and I'm not talking about some mad hatter who's contaminated the candy supply. I'm talking about the poison that is inherent in the sugar-laced, nutrient deficient, non-food product called candy.

It's really kind of bizarre when you think about it. Most loving parents would never let their children ingest poisonous substances that will seriously damage their health, but they don't think twice about allowing them, and even encouraging them, to pump their bodies full of sugared-up candy, which essentially does the same thing in the long run.

When our children eat sugar, they are ingesting a substance that not only results in tooth decay, but also leads to insulin resistance, type 2 diabetes, obesity, acne, heart disease, ADHD, cancer, high blood pressure, anxiety disorders, microbial overgrowth, depression and addiction to name only a few.

Let's get one thing straight—candy is not a real food. It is a conglomerate of food dyes, preservatives, chemicals, and mind-altering substances. Sugar and many of the chemicals in candy impact the brain in the same manner as alcohol and hard drugs like cocaine. It's like handing our children a needle and watching them shoot up. Sugar addiction is rampant in our society and is often the gateway to addiction to harder substances.

On top of that, collecting as much candy as possible and hoarding it away encourages gluttonous behavior that could lead to a life-long pattern of overeating, food addiction, and binging. I mean really, there is no need for all that candy. Americans spend over 2 billion dollars in Halloween candy each year. Wow, that's really frightening. Is this really the kind of behavior we want to teach our children? I don't think so.

On the other hand, you don't want your child to feel deprived or to miss out on the spirit of this ghoulish holiday completely. There are a variety of fun ways to participate in this holiday without destroying the health of your children and neighbors or encouraging addiction, gluttony, overeating, etc.

Find alternatives for your children, like having your own Halloween party and serving just a few healthy treats. When my son was a child, sometimes I would buy a "small" plastic pumpkin and fill it with healthier candy from the health food store like trail mix, gluten-free and fruit juice sweetened cookies, chewing gum sweetened with xylitol, or date cookies. I would probably throw in a couple of non-food items like a Hot Wheels car and a new book as well.

Alternatively, some times we would go to the health food store and I would let him pick out the healthy treats he would like to have. We kept the number of items to around five or six, not an entire bag, and he had to save a couple of them for the following day. Once treats were in hand, then we would go do something special like go to the movies, the arcade, or the mall. He would have his choice. Some years we visited the local haunted house or went on a haunted hay ride. Of course, we also participated in the traditional pumpkin carving and sometimes we roasted pumpkin seeds. Use your imagination and I'm sure you can come up with some ideas of your own.

Now, on the other side of the coin, in addition to taking care of our own children, we also don't want to participate in filling up the trick or treaters that arrive at our door with unhealthy treats. Instead of candy, you can give away cool looking pencils or erasers, trail mix without sugar added, small boxes of raisins, apples, dates, pumpkin seeds, fruit leather made of 100% juice, bananas, oranges, apples, or beef jerky.

Finding some healthy Halloween snacks for our kids not only allows those of us living a holistic life to participate in this fun holiday in a manner that makes us feel good about ourselves, but ensures we will be instilling our children with natural health values that will protect their health now and in the future and teaches them to exercise self-control in the face of sugar and other unhealthy foods.

Again, don't feel guilty for protecting your children. You will be teaching them to engage in healthy eating habits and encouraging a value system that will benefit their emotional and physical health—two of the greatest treats we can give our children.

Valentine's Day

Unfortunately, Valentine's Day is intricately connected with the indulgence of sugar, chocolate, and alcohol, three of the most destructive substances one can consume, especially when they are dealing with candida and its associated conditions.

Once you've made the transition to healthy paleo eating and have a strong foundation to stand on, you won't be so easily influenced by these temptations, but if you're new to a sugar-free diet, the pressure from social conditioning and impairment in brain chemistry and the endocrine system can make it difficult to resist.

Although the world won't come to an end if you succumb for just one day, the problem is that it is very difficult for most people to get back on track, and one day turns into one week, two months, or even a year. When you feed a sugar, chocolate, or alcohol craving, it becomes bigger, more powerful, and difficult to reign back in, because the consumption of these substances incites cravings for more. It is throwing fuel on the fire. Additionally, the price you pay in symptoms is really not worth a few moments of satisfaction.

Furthermore, the development of new and healthier eating habits requires consistency and repetition. Therefore, you are better off in the long run if you begin to build new holiday traditions that do not include the use of sugar, chocolate, or alcohol.

It's really sad that our society programs us to believe that one of the best ways to express our love is to shower our beloved with poisons that will destroy their mental and physical health. There are much better ways to show someone that we love them, and here are some ideas to get your creative juices flowing.

Begin by reminding yourself that the true meaning of Valentine's Day is about celebrating the love you share with your significant other, friend, child, sibling, parent, and yourself, not about sugar, chocolate, and alcohol. Design your celebration so that it focuses on the relationship, not on food and drink. Spend quality time together and express how you feel verbally. There is nothing more powerful than the simple words, "I Love You," followed by an authentic hug.

You can take a walk together or go on a hike in the park, watch a movie, go to the mall or bookstore, make arts and crafts in the kitchen, give or get a massage, visit the playground or arcade, play darts, Uno, Yahtzee, or another game. When my son was a child, we would make our own Valentine's Day cards each year out of construction paper and crayons; it was great fun and the cards were much more meaningful.

Be sure that all your loved ones know that you are committed to healthy eating and that it doesn't involve the consumption of sugar, alcohol, and chocolate. Make it clear that you no longer desire to receive these kinds of gifts. Jewelry, books, a beautiful piece of art, knickknacks, organic flowers or plants, or even a helping hand with the chores can all make a fantastic replacement.

Instead of a box of chocolates, you can give or receive cherries drizzled with almond butter, dates stuffed with almonds, strawberries dipped in walnut butter and sprinkled with coconut flakes. It's really easy to make a wide variety of candy-like treats with coconut butter and your favorite nut butter and a spice like cinnamon or vanilla and the recipe for these can be found further ahead.

Don't have time to invest in making your own healthy treats, trail mix will always do; and a company called Blue Mountain Organics has three delicious flavors (pecan, tropical, and ginger) of a product called Love Bites. Love Bites are a mixture of fruit, nuts, and spices with no added sweeteners; and all their nuts are sprouted.

If you want to simulate a chocolate experience, you can use carob instead. Although carob is a legume, which means it contains anti-nutrients and a fair amount of carbs, and should not be used on a daily basis, it is okay for an occasional cheat and a much better choice than chocolate. Be sure to use roasted carob, since cooking legumes reduces some of their antinutrients. You'll find a recipe for carob fudge on page 172 and my almond thumbprint cookies on page 150 would work just as well too.

Be sure to take some of these treats with you throughout the day, if you think you will be tempted at work or other social situations. Make sure that co-workers are aware that you don't eat sugar, chocolate, etc., as well. Don't be ashamed to stand for healthy eating. Be proud.

And remember, don't feel guilty for restricting sugar and chocolate from your children in your home. You can't control what goes on in other situations, but you can and should control what takes place in your own home. Your home should be a sugar-free zone even on the holidays. Protecting the health of your children and teaching them how to make good food choices is one of the most loving acts you can provide as a parent.

If you go out to eat, then it is easy enough to choose items on the menu that won't completely derail you (meat and low-starch vegetables) and simply skip the sugared-up, chocolaty desserts, and alcoholic beverages. You can have dessert at home or take something you made at home with you. Alternatively, you can cook a paleo approved meal in your own kitchen.

There is no reason you can't, or shouldn't, celebrate the love for your self in the same manner. You deserve it! If you are celebrating Valentine's Day alone, then everything on this page still applies. Be your own Valentine.

Christmas and Easter

Although the holidays may be one of those times when you just can't resist indulging in something delicious and sweet, you can replace those holiday recipes calling for sugar with healthier sugar-free alternatives found in this book. There's a whole section for paleo approved candies, a carrot cake, several cookie recipes, cobbler, carob fudge, and even egg nog. The I'm in Nirvana Sweet Potato recipe on page 128 is as delicious as a piece of pie.

Keep in mind that sugar-free replacements are a healthier choice, but even the desserts in this book should be eaten in moderation. Try not to overindulge and keep their presence in your diet to these special occasions.

By switching to sugar-free holiday desserts, you'll have a healthier and happier holiday and feel better on the days that follow, instead of having a sugar hangover.

Remember that sugar and overeating do not have to be part of your holiday tradition. Put a greater value on the "experience" of the holiday rather than the food.

FORGIVE TRANSGRESSIONS AND MOVE ON

Do not beat yourself up, criticize, belittle, shame, or punish if you give in or fall down. This type of response will only throw fuel on the fire for cravings and make getting back on track more difficult, by lowering your self-esteem and provoking guilt and self-hatred. Changing your diet, like any other form of change, is a process not an event. Setbacks and struggle are a normal part of this process. The consequences you experience when you give in to temptation will help motivate you and make you stronger the next time. At some point, the consequences will begin to outweigh any reward or pleasure you derive from consuming these foods, and setbacks will occur less often and eventually become a thing of the past.

Forgive, let it go, and keep moving forward. Don't let one brief lapse in judgement turn into days, weeks, or months of cheating or binging. However, this does not mean you give yourself permission to cheat or binge—you should still strive for self-discipline and consistency—but you are supportive and kind if you don't. There is a very fine line between acceptance of where you are in the process and giving yourself permission to engage in destructive eating and this line is easy to cross.

IT'S MORE THAN A DIET

You are not going "on" a diet. You are transforming your values, identity, beliefs, and manner in which you live. Long-term success with the ability to be compliant and reap the many rewards that changes in diet offers requires that you create a whole new lifestyle that supports health. In order to sustain improvements in health and remain free of cravings for sugar and carbs, these changes will be life-long, not something you will do for a period of time.

REMAIN COMPLIANT

Once cravings disappear and you begin to feel better, do not return to eating the sugar, carbs, caffeine, chocolate, etc. If you eat these foods again, it is only a matter of time before symptoms and cravings return, because they will disrupt the endocrine system and brain chemistry again. You may get away with an occasional transgression without too many consequences, but non-compliance events should be few and far between. Your changes in diet are permanent, not something you will do for a period of time.

Although the average person may be able to follow the 80/20 or 85/15 rule for diet compliance that is often recommended by paleo experts, that is not the case for the person who has an addiction to sugar, carbs, caffeine, chocolate, grains, etc. You will need to remain compliant 98 percent of the time. In some cases, it may require 100 percent compliance or the individual relapses and finds themselves binging on their food or foods of choice. Just like an alcohol addicted individual who can never have just one drink, because it always leads to more drinks, the same is true for the sugar and carb addicted. In order to remain free of cravings for sugar and carbs you simply don't eat them.

What About Those Other Paleo Cookbooks?

Many people who end up at my doorstep are already familiar with the paleo way of eating and may have acquired a variety of paleo cookbooks along the way. They are sometimes confused and question me as to why my recipes don't include some of the ingredients they commonly see in other paleo/primal cookbooks like fermented foods, bone broth, apple cider vinegar, balsamic vinegar, chocolate, coffee, green tea, bacon, or breakfasts that include fruit, nuts, kefir and yogurt or pastries (cookies, cakes, pancakes, breads, pie) made from almond flour and other moderately high-carb meals with paleo approved carbs.

Please be aware that most paleo/primal cookbooks on the market are designed for the general population, not for the person who has candida, SIBO, sugar and carb addiction, and all the conditions that typically accompany these issues like insulin resistance, carbohydrate intolerance, sympathetic nervous system dominance, adrenal fatigue, blood sugar issues, sleep disturbances, fibromyalgia, anxiety and depression, histamine intolerance, glutamate excess, etc. I have taken the basic paleo principles and tweaked them for the individual who is dealing with these issues. People who don't have these conditions can get away with consumption of these foods, but you do not have that same luxury.

Additionally, you should be aware that addiction is alive and well in the paleo community and many people just replace their traditional addictions (sugar, wheat, etc.) with paleo approved addictive foods. It is very common for me to work with people who are addicted to or binging on nuts, seeds, coconut butter, pastries made from almond flour, fruit, dates, figs, sweet potatoes, dark chocolate, and coffee.

As we learned in the *Healing Chronic Candida* book, bone broth, cultured or fermented foods (including coconut aminos) are both very high in histamine and glutamate and the individual with candida and/ or SIBO tend to have excess levels of histamine and glutamate already. If they eat foods that are high in these substances, then it increases their elevation even more, contributing to a wide array of symptoms and further deterioration in health. In my experience, most people with candida overgrowth do not tolerate these foods, so I see no reason to include them in the diet plan. Additionally, these foods can be problematic for the individual with SIBO as well.

As discussed in great depth in *Healing Chronic Candida*, chocolate and coffee (or other caffeinated substances) are addictive mind-altering drugs that impair brain chemistry and the endocrine system, cause nutritional deficiencies, promote sympathetic dominance, and fuel cravings for sugar and carbs that sabotage one's ability to remain compliant with their diet. Chocolate or raw cacao contain an abundance of psychotropic substances that can affect the brain in a similar manner as alcohol, marijuana, heroin, cocaine, and amphetamines all at the same time, leading to depletion of critical neurotransmitters like dopamine, serotonin, endorphins, GABA, and endocannabinoids. Chocolate also increases glutamate and is high in histamine, oxalates, phytates, and mycotoxins. Coffee contains a morphine-like substance called cafestol that depletes endorphins, it is also high in mold toxins and histamine, and causes inflammation and permeability of the gut. Additionally, coffee and chocolate are not true paleo, but many paleo/primal people make an exception for them. They are often referred to in the paleo/ primal community as a "sensible indulgence." However, for people with candida, SIBO, adrenal fatigue, sympathetic nervous system dominance, sugar and carb addiction, or any other addiction, this would not be sensible. This is also true even if the coffee is combined with butter or some other source of fat that is encouraged by many in the paleo world— it does not change the fact that caffeine is an addictive mind-altering drug that lowers levels of acetylcholine, GABA, and serotonin, depletes vital nutrients like iron, zinc, potassium, calcium, vitamin D, B1, inositol, and biotin, impairs one's ability to maintain balance in blood glucose levels, and perpetuates excess sympathetic nervous system activity. The same is true for chocolate in the paleo society that has reduced levels of mold.

Although fruit and nuts can be nutritious in moderation for the healthy person, they can contribute to overgrowth of microbes, degradation of gut health, sympathetic dominance, impairment of brain chemistry and endocrine function, and burden adrenals in the candida population, all of which lead to symptoms like depression, anxiety, headaches, low blood sugar, and cravings for sugar and carbs, thus again, undermining your ability to stay committed to your diet.

While pastries (cakes, cookies, pancakes, pie, breads) made from almond flour are certainly a better choice than wheat or other grains, nuts oxidize and produce free radicals when they are cooked, so not something we want to do on a frequent basis. Nuts can be problematic for other reasons, when eaten in excess. For example, they are too high in omega-6 that lead to more inflammation, antinutrients that impair absorption of minerals, can be a food source for many microbes, and may prompt an immune response. You can avoid the oxidizing issue by using coconut flour or chestnut flour, but the way the ingredients are combined for making pastries still creates an end product that can be too high in carbs and feed microbes, also leading to abandonment of the diet. So any type of "paleo" pastry should be used sparingly in the diet and reserved for special occasions like holidays or birthdays or a special treat.

Again, high-carb foods that are paleo approved, (e.g. sweet potatoes, yams, winter squash, taro, etc.) are acceptable for the general population, but for the individual with candida, sugar and carb addiction, carb intolerance, and all the aforementioned conditions like adrenal fatigue and sympathetic dominance, it will feed the microbes and fuel cravings for more sugar and carbs. These foods, can be eaten on rare occasion, but not a regular basis. If you eat high-carb foods, you will crave carbs, even those that are paleo approved. Additionally, all carbs (even paleo approved) feed candida and other pathogenic microbes.

Anything fermented (cultured vegetables, apple cider vinegar, balsamic vinegar) has a small amount of alcohol. This could be a trigger for cravings for any addictive substance like alcohol, sugar, carbs, and caffeine, especially in early phases of recovery. All fermented food is high in glutamate and histamine as well, so it is problematic if these are already elevated. Ferments may also trigger allergic-like reactions in people with candida, due to their similarity to yeast.

A similar issue arises around the issue of raw vs cooked food. People with severe gut inflammation, which is typically the case within the candida population, do best with the majority of their food cooked soft. Cooked food is also better for adrenal fatigue, which commonly accompanies candida, as it takes more energy to digest raw food than it does cooked food. If SIBO is involved, then it is vital that food is cooked soft to reduce the food source (fiber and resistant starch) for bacteria. Cooking also reduces some of the antinutrient content that can be found in some foods and lowers oxalate levels and goitrogens. As we learned in the first *Healing Chronic Candida* book, many nutrients are increased when food is cooked, additionally cooking food enabled us to develop bigger brains and advance as a species. So, there is no harm in eating cooked food.

Vinegar is best avoided as it usually triggers an allergic-like reaction in people with candida. Additionally, vinegar is made by fermenting alcohol into acetic acid. Although most manufacturers claim there is no alcohol left, the truth is that there may be trace amounts of alcohol, which can be a trigger for cravings for alcohol, caffeine, sugar and carbs, or other addictive substances in some people. It is also high in glutamate and histamine. This includes apple cider vinegar and balsamic vinegar. However, if you do indulge in vinegar once in a while, it should be apple cider or balsamic and not grain based vinegar.

Yes, I know, it is almost a sin to be paleo and not be a bacon lover. However, I don't encourage the consumption of pork, because it contains parasites. It is my opinion that this is a risk that people with candida and other gut issues are better avoiding. Therefore, you will not find any recipes in this book that contain pork. However, if you think I'm being too paranoid about the parasite issue and wish to include pork in your diet, then it is paleo approved and a good source of animal protein and fat, that shouldn't have any other negative effects on candida or SIBO.

I'm not trying to discourage you from using other paleo cookbooks. There are many superb choices on the market that will be a great addition to your pantry and you should own some of them. Just be aware of which ingredients should be avoided for your purpose and replace with a substitution or eliminate. Don't assume that every recipe in a paleo cookbook will be suitable for you just because it is paleo.

Gauging Your Carb Intake and Other Things to Consider

As mentioned in the opening chapter, the meal plans later in this book include one dessert option for those who are eating within the 60 to 70 grams of carbs per day category. If you are in the group of people who do better staying below 50 grams, then simply ignore the dessert option. All meals in the meal plan and main course meal recipes will keep you below 50 grams of carbs per day, if the dessert option is not included. If you need to be below the 25 or 30 grams per day, then you'll also need to keep your servings of vegetables on the small side, in addition to skipping the dessert.

There are a few recipes in the dessert section that will not take you over the 50 grams per day, which include Dairy-Free Whipped Cream, The Real Deal Whipped Cream, Sunflower Macaroons, Vanilla Almond Butter, Pumpkin Pie Mousse, Paleo Approved Candies, Nuts and Cream, Coconut Pops, Ice Cream Bites, Pumpkin and Pecan Ice Cream, Carob Cream, and Easy Bake Cookies. The carb content of each of these lower carb options is indicated in the recipe itself. So, if you'd like a dessert and need to remain below 50, then you can include those options. Additionally, some of the other desserts may be possible to eat without going over 50, if you eat a very small serving. However, if you aren't able to go above 25 or 30, this will not be an option. Use the carb charts at the end of the book to monitor your carb intake for vegetables, fruits, nuts and seeds.

If you include the dessert option in your menu, it is your choice on which meal it will be added to, but be aware that it is best to not eat carbs too close to bedtime, because they are too stimulating, which may disrupt the sleep cycle. Carbs consumed at night can result in a drop in blood sugar in the middle of the night, which results in setting off the stress response system and that means an elevation in cortisol and norepinephrine, which will wake you up and may produce a variety of symptoms like fear, anxiety, restlessness, agitation, headaches, racing heart, and more. Additionally, insulin (which is released if you eat carbs) interferes with melatonin production, the hormone needed for inducing sleep. It is animal protein and fat before bed that will prevent dips in blood sugar and encourage a peaceful night's sleep.

Fruit, nuts, seeds, or any other high-carb paleo food should never be eaten on an empty stomach, used as a snack, or as the main course meal, they should always be consumed after the main course meal to decrease their impact on blood sugar, neurotransmitters, and insulin. Animal protein and fat should be used as snacks.

As we learned in *Healing Chronic Candida* book one, your carb intake should be gauged by the amount and severity of symptoms and cravings that are produced when carbs are eaten. If you are still experiencing cravings for sugar or carbs and/or a lot of symptoms (anxiety, headaches, crashing later, itching, depression, irritability, impaired cognitive functions, etc.) with the carbs you are eating, then you are still eating too many. The desire for carbs simply disappears when you stop consuming them and overgrowth symptoms will diminish. Your goal is to lower your intake of carbs below the threshold that produces symptoms and cravings. This can vary widely from individual to individual, (zero to 25 grams for one, 50 for another, or 70 for another or anything in between) so you have to find what is right for your body. Additionally, your threshold can change throughout your lifetime in response to other factors like age, stage of life, stress levels, exposure to toxins, degree of metabolic damage, level of physical activity, other health conditions that may exist, and where you are in the healing process, so it frequently needs to be assessed and adjusted.

As your level of overgrowth is reduced, gut health improves, and you restore balance to brain chemistry and the endocrine system, then your threshold for paleo approved carbs may improve. There may be a period of time where you can't tolerate hardly any carbs in any form, but later in your healing journey you can. However, once one becomes carbohydrate intolerant, as is the case for most people who have had candida for a long time, this typically does not go away completely. The severity of metabolic damage will determine how much this changes. At least to some degree, the carbs are going to be restricted for life and most people should not go above the 60 to 70 grams on a regular basis at any point to maintain the improvements in health they achieve and keep cravings for sugar and carbs from returning. You may get away with an occasional splurge up around 100 or so for a birthday or holiday, but that is not something that should be done frequently.

If you happen to be in the category of people who tolerates 60 to 70 grams of carbs per day with no problem, but you are overweight or trying to lose weight, then you will likely want to go below the 50 grams per day anyhow, at least for a period of time. Initially it will help you transition more smoothly and quickly from a sugar burner to a fat burner, which leads to weight loss. It may be difficult to get the body to become a fat burner instead of a sugar burner with the consumption of 60 to 70 grams per day in some people. Alternatively, you may be able to go up around 60 to 70 two or three times a week, if you stay below 50 the other four or five days. This is especially true for postmenopausal women. Once you make the transition and your body is good at burning fat, then you may be able to go up to the 60 to 70, but for some, the weight comes back on if they don't remain below 50. Generally speaking, we become less tolerant of carbohydrates as we age, and the changes in hormones and metabolism that occur after menopause changes the way we respond to carbohydrates.

Additionally, you may find that you can eat one particular serving size of fruit, nuts, or other paleo approved higher carb food, but not another. At most, serving size of these carbs should not exceed a half cup or so, but that may be too much for some people. However, these individuals may be able to get away with a quarter cup. A whole banana, apple, peach, pear, or sweet potato may trigger cravings and an avalanche of symptoms for some, but a half of one of either of these, or one in particular, may be acceptable. You may not tolerate fruit at all in its raw state, but may be able to do a serving if it is cooked soft.

Combining your fruit or other high-carb food with fat will reduce its glycemic index, which means less impact on neurotransmitters, blood sugar, and insulin and consequently less negative symptoms and cravings. Additionally, your fruit and nuts should be eaten after your main course meal, not alone, for the same reasons. For example, I can't eat fruit unless it is eaten after my main course meal and combined with a significant amount of fat (heavy cream, coconut cream, nuts, seeds, coconut butter). The more fat, the better my tolerance. Thus, you will notice that all desserts in this book are rich in fat, so you don't have to figure it out yourself.

The same is true for nuts, you may not tolerate any nuts in their raw state, but do okay with a small amount of lightly roasted nuts. Whole nuts may produce a vast array of symptoms, but nut butter may be doable. A half cup of nuts may cause inflammation of the gut and trigger cravings for carbs, but a quarter cup could be just right. Two tablespoons of nut butter may generate symptoms, but one teaspoon may not. It may also be a matter of frequency, you may be able to eat fruit or nuts once or twice a week without symptoms or trigger for cravings, but not every day.

Experiment and play around with ratios and timing of carbs to find what works best for you. Since many foods that must be reduced can be health enhancing, then be sure to challenge yourself periodically to see if your threshold has changed, but don't go above the 60 to 70 grams per day.

I haven't provided any recipes that include oranges, tangerines, melons, or cantaloupes, because these foods are so high in mold and they typically provoke a variety of symptoms in most people with candida. However, if you happen to tolerate these foods, then feel free to add them if you like. I also stayed away from pineapple in most cases, as it is quite offensive for the individual with SIBO. But, again, if you tolerate pineapple, it can be substituted in many of the recipes on occasion.

For more diversity in your diet and to avoid boredom, be creative with your dessert options by preparing and serving them in different ways. Your fruit experience can be completely different depending on whether it is fresh, frozen, whole, sliced, chopped, mashed, or crushed into a sorbet. The same is true for nuts and seeds, which can be eaten in their whole state or chopped, ground into meal, or made into nut butter. Each of these options provides you with an end result that is somewhat unique in flavor and texture. Spices like cinnamon, nutmeg, and vanilla can be added for more adventure. For example, a peach could be sliced fresh and dipped into pecan butter, or it could be baked with chopped pecans on top of it, or frozen and put in the blender with whole pecans. Either of those peach options would taste different with cinnamon, nutmeg, or vanilla. A sweet potato can be baked like a regular potato, made into french fries, or sliced and fried.

NUTS AND SEEDS

Nuts and seeds contain some degree of carbohydrate content, that will feed candida and other microbes with some having higher levels than others. So they must be considered in your total carbohydrate intake for the day. Cashews, chestnuts, pistachios, and chia seeds contain the most carbs, while walnuts, Brazil nuts, pecans, macadamia nuts, pine nuts, pumpkin seeds, and sunflower seeds are lowest. Additionally, the fiber content of nuts and seeds can be a significant source of food for SIBO. Nuts and seeds can also be somewhat moldy, which incites symptoms for the mold sensitive. You may want to note that the macadamia nut is lower in mold than others and the pistachio is higher in mold than others. Peanuts are not a nut, they are a legume. Since legumes should not be part of the diet due to their antinutrient content and ability to contribute to leaky gut, inflammation, and autoimmune disorders, the peanut should not be eaten. There is not agreement in the field whether cashews are a true paleo food or not. Cashews are actually toxic if eaten raw. All cashews that you buy in a store have been cooked to some degree even if it states they are raw. The cashew has to be processed in a particular manner in order to remove its toxins before it is fit for consumption. Additionally, cashews are actually a fruit and not a nut. They are also higher in carb and tend to be addictive for most people with sugar and carb addiction issues. Therefore, you will not find them in any of the recipes in this book as a main ingredient. An occasional indulgence in some cashews probably not a big deal, but one should not eat them on a regular basis.

Most nuts and seeds also contain a significant level of poly-unsaturated fats (PUFAs) (with the exception of the macadamia and chestnut) and most of that is omega-6. This can contribute to an imbalance in the omega-6 to omega-3 ratio if nuts and seeds are eaten too frequently in large amounts. Although omega-6 is critical for health, it results in inflammation when in excess, which would then contribute to poor gut health and perpetuate candida overgrowth and can then lead to all the conditions associated with inflammation like neurological disorders, cardiovascular disease, type 2 diabetes, autoimmune disorders, obesity, etc. However, even too much omega-3 can be harmful, as it may be associated with an increased risk in colitis and changes in immune function that may impair the body's ability to fight off microbes like candida and bacteria.[2] So, you don't want to go overboard there either. Additionally, when we are eating low-carb, the body prefers saturated and monounsaturated fat. You'll note in the charts on page 194 that the macadamia is very rich in monounsaturated fats (MUFA) and low in PUFA. Pecans and hazelnuts are also a good source of MUFA, but have more PUFA than macadamia. Chia seeds, pine nuts, and walnuts are very low in MUFA and quite high in PUFA. Although walnuts are high in omega-3, they are even higher in omega-6. The fat, protein, minerals, flavonoids, and antioxidants that are present in nuts and seeds counteract some of the PUFA impact, as long as they are being consumed sensibly.

It is true that flax and chia seeds are higher in omega-3 than omega-6. However, the omega-3 content that is present in nuts and seeds (Alpha linoleic acid, or ALA) must be converted into DHA and EPA in order to be useful for our body, and most people do not make this conversion very effectively. Therefore, nuts and seeds are not a good source of omega-3 anyhow. Your omega-3 content is best obtained from grass-fed beef and buffalo, wild fish, and omega-3 rich eggs.

Additionally, the flax seed is high in phytoestrogens, that can mimic human estrogen, contributing to estrogen dominance and all the problems associated with this situation, like making candida proliferate, cravings for sugar and carbs, explosive anger or rage, headaches, intense irritability, depression, anxiety, and mood swings, so I think it is best to avoid flax altogether.

You'll also find a substantial amount of phytates in nuts and seeds, the antinutrient that can attach to minerals in your gastrointestinal tract and impede your ability to utilize them. Phytates may also irritate and inflame the gut, decrease activity of some digestive enzymes, and prompt an immune response, which means they can contribute to autoimmune disorders, leaky gut, and nutritional deficiencies, if eaten too frequently or in excess. Nuts and seeds contain some degree of lectins and protease inhibitors that can contribute to leaky gut or impaired digestion if eaten in excess as well. Most nuts and seeds are also somewhat high in histamine or tyramine content, so they can be problematic for the individual who is sensitive to these substances. The macadamia and chestnut are much lower in phytates than others.

The body can handle some degree of phytates without problems (usually about 100 to 400 mg per day), so as long as you have removed other foods that are high in phytate (grains, legumes, and chocolate) and consume a moderate amount of nuts and seeds, the phytate aspect should not be too much of an issue for a healthy individual. However, the person with a damaged gut is more vulnerable, so they should soak their nuts and seeds prior to eating them, which can significantly reduce the phytate content. Place your nuts or seeds in a bowl and cover with water. Soak overnight for about 12 hours. Pour the water off and pat them dry with a paper towel. Put them in the fridge or the freezer for longer keeping. Alternatively, you could put them in a dehydrator. If you don't have time for all this, there's a great company called Blue Mountain Organics that carries an entire line of soaked nuts and seeds and their respective butters. Nuts and nut butters should always be stored in the refrigerator to inhibit mold growth and prevent oxidation.

For these reasons, consumption of nuts and seeds should be limited for the person with candida, SIBO, and the associated conditions like sugar and carb addiction, adrenal fatigue, leaky gut, IBS, and autoimmune disorders. Ideally, they probably shouldn't be eaten every day and should never be used as the main course meal. The SIBO individual may need to avoid them altogether, if overgrowth is severe. When you do eat nuts and seeds, be cognizant of their PUFA, MUFA, and carb content and try to choose those that are highest in MUFA (monounsaturated fat) content and lowest in carb most frequently. Indulge in the ones with high PUFA and carb on a less frequent basis. The chart on page 194, provides you with this data. Considering that the macadamia is low in carb, rich in monounsaturated fat, low in PUFA, and has less mold and phytates, it is the healthiest nut you can eat overall.

Roasting your nuts and seeds will reduce their mold content and lower the fiber available for SIBO to ferment. However, heating a nut or seed oxidizes its PUFAs, which makes them rancid and leads to the development of free radicals and toxins that can harm our cells like "advanced lipid oxidation endproducts" (ALEs), or lipid peroxides, which cause inflammation. The more PUFA they contain, the more susceptible they are to oxidation. But, the extent of oxidation is also affected by vitamin E and flavonoid content that can provide some protection, how long it is subjected to the heat, and temperature. Therefore, roasting or cooking a nut or seed in any way is not something we want to do frequently. When you do, choose the nuts that have lower levels of PUFA, keep the temperature lower, roast for a short period of time and be sure to stick with dry roasted, as they are less vulnerable than those coated in oil. Nuts and seeds are also vulnerable to oxidation in the presence of light and air, so keep them stored in a dark area in an air tight container.

Chestnuts are unique as far as nuts go, because unlike most nuts, they are not high in fat, they are more carb. As mentioned above they have very little PUFA and are lower in phytates. Since they are high in carbs, they can't be consumed liberally. However, they are fine for the occasional treat and if you have a need for a little more carb in your diet for one reason or another, then they make a good paleo approved option. Since they are low in PUFA, they can be roasted, baked, boiled, etc. and used in a variety of recipes. They are great in both sweet and savory dishes like desserts, soups, salads, or meat and vegetable dishes. You can also turn chestnuts into a puree or a flour and use them for baking.

Pistachios are particularly high in prebiotic fiber, meaning they make a good food source for bacteria in the gut.[3] This can be a good thing if you want to increase your friendly flora. However, for the individual with SIBO, which has too much bacteria in the gut, this can exacerbate the issue.

FATS AND OILS

Like the nut and seed itself, oils obtained from these foods are also vulnerable to oxidation by heat, air, and light, and high in PUFAs, but even more so, because isolating the oil from the nut or seed strips it of other naturally occurring substances that may provide some protection from these elements and minimize the impact of high PUFAs. Therefore, oils derived from nuts and seeds should be consumed minimally.

The only fats that should be used for high-heat cooking are coconut oil, ghee, and butter. If you want oil on your food, then add it after it is cooked. Oils that can be used cold, include walnut oil, sesame oil, olive oil, macadamia oil, avocado oil, and high-oleic sunflower oil. Be sure to note there is a difference between sunflower oil and "high oleic" sunflower oil. You want to avoid the former, because it is higher in omega-6. I don't encourage the use of lard, since it is derived from pork, which I mentioned on page 43 that I suggest avoiding due to parasite contamination. However, if you choose to include pork, then lard can be used for cooking as well. Beef tallow and duck fat are acceptable as well.

Like the nut, macadamia oil is higher in MUFAs, walnut oil is very high in PUFAS. So be careful how often you use the oils that are high in PUFA. High consumption of oil high in PUFA can cause a serious imbalance in omega-6 to omega-3 ratio. Use the nut and seed chart on page 194, if the nut is high in PUFA, its oil will be as well.

All oil should be expeller pressed, meaning no chemicals like hexane are used in the process; and cold pressed, meaning it is not exposed to high heat that will cause oxidation, which also preserves flavor, aroma, and nutritional content. Olive oil should contain the words "extra virgin" meaning it has been expeller and cold pressed, and it should also contain the words "first pressed." Pressing the olive more than once results in less flavor, acidity, and nutritional value. However, it's important to be aware that fraud in the olive oil industry is rampant. Studies have found that a large percentage of the olive oil in the market is adulterated or fake. Olive oil may be replaced or diluted with another cheaper oil, so be sure to buy a reputable brand.

Like the nut, oils should be stored in a cool dark place to prevent oxidation and they should be used within a reasonable amount of time. If it takes you awhile to get through a bottle of oil, then buy a small bottle.

Fat plays a significant role in a low-carb diet. Generally speaking, the lower the carb intake, the higher the need for fat, because fat will be your primary source of energy. You should consume as much fat as needed to feel satiated. Since our culture has demonized fat for decades, this can be difficult to accept at first and it may seem like you are eating a ridiculous amount of fat. As mentioned previously, when eating low-carb, the body prefers saturated and monounsaturated fat. Most of your fat should come from animal sources, and then it can be supplemented with things like olives, avocados, nuts, and coconut.

BUTTER, GHEE, AND HEAVY CREAM

Although butter, ghee, and heavy cream are not an inherent component of paleo, they are good sources of fat and have little to no carb content. Therefore, if you are not dairy intolerant, or they do not incite cravings or trigger you to binge, and you don't have an autoimmune disorder, they are acceptable. However, for those who wish to remain 100 percent true to paleo principles, then most of the recipes in this book that contain butter, ghee, or heavy cream will provide an alternative. If you consistently stay below the 50 grams of carbs per day, you will likely find it is difficult to avoid the butter, ghee, or heavy cream, as your need for fat will be significantly higher. Yogurt is a good source of fat as well, but it contains lactose, which will feed candida and other microbes. Therefore, it cannot be eaten as freely as butter, ghee, and heavy cream and you will only find one recipe in this book with yogurt. Greek yogurt is made by straining the whey, which results in higher protein and less lactose, so it is the best choice. But, yogurt can be problematic for the individual with high glutamate and in some cases high histamine, depending on the microbes used in fermentation; and for the individual with SIBO, if overgrowth involves friendly bacteria.

SALT

When we eat low-carb, there is a greater need for salt, because the body eliminates salt more effectively in the absence of carbs.[4] Additionally, salt is vital for proper functioning of the adrenal glands and delivering vitamin C to the adrenals, which are weak in most people with candida. It is also critical for managing sympathetic nervous system activity and proper transmission of neurotransmitters. Therefore, all recipes in this book contain salt. If you have a need for lower salt intake, then naturally you can just eliminate this ingredient.

However, traditional table salt should be avoided, because it consists of nothing but sodium chloride, has been stripped of vital nutrients, and contains additives that are not health promoting. Salt should be pink or gray in color and course. It is often referred to as rock salt, Himalayan salt, or Celtic salt. I prefer a brand called Real Salt™. Salt is discussed in greater detail in the *Healing Chronic Candida* book.

WATER

We also eliminate water more effectively when we eat low-carb, so water intake may need to be increased as well.[5] It should be free of chlorine and other toxins.

STEVIA

Stevia will not increase blood glucose levels or feed candida or other pathogenic microbes. In most cases, it does not incite cravings for sugar and carbs. However, on a rare occasion, I do work with someone who gets addicted to stevia. When we eat something that is sweet on the palate, the body thinks it is about to get some sugar, so it may respond accordingly. If the consumption of stevia triggers cravings for sugar and carbs, or you find yourself binging on stevia sweetened baked goods, then it would need to be eliminated. Sometimes it is a temporary problem due to severe metabolic damage that may improve once the endocrine system begins to regain some balance. Again, this seems to be a problem in a very minor part of the population. Most people eat stevia with no negative effects. Some studies have shown that stevia improves insulin sensitivity, lowers blood glucose, and inhibits biofilms.[6]

Even still, the use of stevia should be done in moderation. Your goal in reducing sugar and carb consumption is to eliminate your desire for sweets, not replace them with something else. So, you will find that I use stevia in some of the recipes in this book, but it is used sparingly. In most cases, you want to learn to appreciate the level of sweetness that is present in a food in its natural state.

Additionally, it is critical to avoid the stevia known as Truvia, which is sold in traditional grocery stores, because it is not true stevia. This is a combination of stevia and erythritol. Besides the fact that erythritol can cause great GI distress and feed SIBO, the erythritol used in the main stream food supply has been obtained from genetically modified corn, which has been shown to contain high levels of the toxic herbicide known as Roundup or glyphosate, which has a variety of profound negative effects on the brain, gut, and endocrine system, which can lead to cravings for sugar and carbs and overeating, as well as many other symptoms like depression, and anxiety, and cause more deterioration in gut health and overgrowth of candida. Erythritol with Roundup is so potent that it has been demonstrated to kill fruit files. The more Truvia the fruit flies consumed, the quicker they died.[7] Be sure you purchase organic and pure stevia only.

CAROB

Carob is not a paleo approved food, because it is a legume, which means its antinutrient content could contribute to gut inflammation, nutritional deficiencies, autoimmune disorders, etc. Additionally, it is moderately high in carbs and fiber, which means it will feed candida and SIBO, increase blood sugar, prompt an immune response, and may contribute to cravings for sugar and carbs. However, an occasional indulgence in carob is not going to be too destructive. You will find two recipes in this book that include carob as a primary ingredient, and it is an option in several others. This does not mean it should be consumed daily, or even monthly, but it can be used as an alternative on any of the holidays that typically include chocolate (which should always be avoided), or as a special treat. Just be sure to be sensible about the size of your serving and refrain from frequent consumption. Furthermore, cooking carob will significantly lower some of its lectin content, so be sure to use carob that has been cooked.

Carob is always a better option than chocolate, because it does not contain any of the addictive, mind-altering, autonomic nervous system disrupting chemicals and substances that are present in chocolate. It can be used in any recipe that calls for chocolate, including a hot cup of cocoa. Again, not something you want to do on a regular basis, but a hot cup of carob milk on a cold winter's night once a year as a special treat would not be too damaging in most cases.

SNACKS

Once again, I'd like to call to your attention that the fruit, seeds, and nuts are in the dessert option of the meal plan not the snack option. Contrary to popular belief, snacking should not include foods like fruit, nuts, and seeds, granola, trail mix, or baked goods, even if they are paleo approved. You should also avoid manufactured products labeled as paleo friendly protein bars, energy bars, or snack bars. All these foods are way too high in carbs, which will feed candida and other microbes, provide fuel for cravings, contribute to sympathetic dominance, and inhibit your ability to restore balance to your brain chemistry and endocrine system. Snacks should consist of animal protein and fat. It is animal protein and fat that will keep blood sugar stable and ward off cravings for sugar and carbs.

When you first begin the candida diet, and you are going through the transition from sugar burner to fat burner and your blood sugar will be unstable, then you may need to snack a couple times a day. However, once your endocrine system and brain chemistry are repaired to some degree and you keep carbs out of the diet, the need to snack will disappear. Hunger between meals will not occur when you eat adequate levels of animal protein and fat and reduce the carbs.

If a snack is needed, the simplest and quickest option is to use whatever meat you are eating that day. This can be combined with a small serving of low-carb vegetable if you like, but the most important element is the animal protein and fat. Vegetables should not be used alone for the snack, as they are mostly carb. If you wake in the middle of the night with low blood sugar, then eat animal protein and fat shortly before going to bed. Low blood sugar can be a primary cause of waking up in the middle of the night.

GOOD SNACK OPTIONS

- sugar-free beef jerky (make your own or get from someplace like US Wellness Meats)

- paleo meatballs

- hot dogs (sugar and nitrate free)

- left over omelets

- hard boiled egg with sliced avocado

- cold meat loaf

- sirloin tips

- beef kabobs

- sliced roast beef

- cold burger

- lamb chop

- salmon patty

- chicken leg, thigh, or tenders

- cubed chicken breast

- salami or sausage (free of sugar and nitrates)

- meat sticks (from someplace like US Wellness Meats)

- deli meats (free of sugar and nitrates)

- sliced turkey breast

- any leftover that contains animal protein

Once the necessity for a snack has ended, then it is best to avoid snacking, especially if you have SIBO. Snacking prevents the migrating motor complex from moving bacteria and other debris that should not be in the small intestine into the large intestine. Meals should be no closer than four or five hours apart to allow the migrating motor complex to perform its functions. However, you don't want to go longer than five hours, or blood sugar will likely drop too low.

PREPARATION

No cooking with gas or propane stoves/oven, both of these substances can disrupt brain chemistry, which may lead to overwhelming cravings for sugar and carbs, binging, compulsive overeating, and a wide array of neurological symptoms like depression, anxiety, irritability, unexplained anger, insomnia, and more. This is true of gas heat in your home as well.[8]

No cooking with aluminum or teflon coated pans, as they release a variety of toxic chemicals that deposit in your food that can impair brain chemistry, disrupt the endocrine system, and weaken the immune system, which may trigger cravings for sugar and carbs, binging, and neurological symptoms. Aluminum has been associated with other conditions like Alzheimer's. Use glass, stainless steel, or cast iron cookware.

No cooking in microwaves, they have been shown to significantly lower the nutrient content in food, not to mention the radiation exposure.

Store leftovers, foods in your pantry, etc. in glass as well, not soft plastic, which also releases a variety of chemicals that can impact brain chemistry and the endocrine system the same way.

Avoid canned products as much as possible and choose glass when possible. When you must buy in the can, choose from a manufacturer who states the can is BPA (bisphenol A) free. BPA is an endocrine-disrupting toxin that is correlated with insulin resistance, birth defects, early puberty, miscarriage, damage to DNA, testosterone deficiency, and cancer.

Use unbleached parchment paper and muffin liners to avoid exposure to bleach, which can also alter brain chemistry and kill off friendly flora in the gut.

Be sure the water that you cook with is filtered and free of chlorine and other contaminants that can impair brain chemistry and the endocrine system and sabotage your ability to remain compliant on the diet.

READ LABELS

When you begin eating in a manner that supports your health, it becomes necessary to read labels thoroughly, even in the health food store. A lot of food that can be found in the health food store is far from healthy. Potato chips, cookies, crackers, popcorn, and candy, from the health food store is still junk food. Most gluten-free breads and pastries are still way too high in carbs and typically contain a variety of other undesirable ingredients that can trigger cravings for carbs and sugar or cause neurological symptoms.

The words "spices" or "natural flavoring" can mean many different things, and may contain some type of sugar, a nightshade, or a substance that increases glutamate or histamine.

Many of the sweeteners that the health food industry uses to replace refined white sugar like organic cane sugar, evaporated cane juice, honey, maple syrup, beet sugar, agave, coconut sugar, nectar or syrup, still feed candida and other microbes, promote sugar and carb addiction and lead to conditions like insulin resistance, type 2 diabetes, heart disease and obesity. Things like zylitol, erythritol, and the other "tols" feed SIBO or cause GI distress.

Additionally, there are many substances added to processed meats and dairy in the health food store that can increase glutamate or histamine levels.

Miscellaneous Tidbits

Olives can add flavor and a little extra fat to just about any main course meal and increase its satiation level. Look for olives that are not in a vinegar base. Sea salt or lemon juice would be acceptable. However, for those who are histamine sensitive, you may have to moderate olives.

Avocados will also increase flavor, fat content, and satiation to most meals as well, and can even be used in many desserts without detection to make them richer and more flavorful. However, for those who are histamine sensitive, this may also need moderated.

You can be creative with your spices in your main course meals as well to add more variety and pizzazz to your dishes, if you are able to include spices freely. A change in spice can transform one dish into something completely different and unique.

Steaming is the preferred method of cooking vegetables as they will retain more of their nutrient content and alkalinity. However, if you have excess oxalates, boiling is better for reducing oxalates, until the level is reduced.

Lettuce or steamed cabbage leaves can replace anything that calls for bread, buns, or a pasta wrap of any kind.

Cabbage, broccoli, cauliflower, carrots, and zucchini all taste great with spaghetti sauce, so they make a good replacement for pasta.

If a food needs a lot of alteration to make it fit for consumption, then we need to question whether it is something we should be eating.

If you have SIBO, you may find that your tolerance for fruit is better if you sauté or bake your fruit before using in the recipes.

Although I typically recommend staying away from dried fruit, because it is so high in sugar content, they (dates, raisins, figs, etc.) can be used on occasion for intense sugar and carb cravings. In the initial stages of the diet, when cravings may be frequent, they can be kept on hand. Since they require no preparation before eating, they make a quick fix when cravings come out of nowhere and are overwhelming. Dip them in nut butter or coconut butter to add some fat, which will lower their glycemic index and increase satiation.

Use coconut butter if avoiding nut butter.

When you indulge in dairy, it should be full-fat only.

Gelatin can be used to make a variety of Jell-o-like recipes, but I didn't include any of those recipes, because gelatin is high in glutamate, and many people with candida are high in glutamate. If you aren't, this may be an option for you.

Juice from fruit and vegetables can be used as dye for coloring eggs at Easter, or any other recipe that requires color. For example, cherry juice, beet juice, carrot juice, and kale juice are some good choices for coloring.

Keep well hydrated and increase salt intake when below 50 grams of carbs, as we eliminate both of these more effectively in the absence of carbs. If you feel acidic, a dash of lemon juice in your water can help alkalize.

Cinnamon will lower the glycemic index of a high-carb food, and thus decrease its impact. However, cinnamon incites histamine release, which can be problematic for the individual with excess histamine.

Vinegar has this affect as well, but as discussed on page 43, vinegar is not something the individual with candida should be eating very often.

If blood sugar levels have dropped, butter can be used to bring it back up quickly. Just eat two tablespoons right off the spoon by itself.

Frozen food can be more nutritious than fresh food in some cases, depending on the time period from harvest to plate. When a food is frozen, its nutrient content is locked in and preserved. Fresh food loses nutrient content over time during shipping and sitting on the shelf.

EATING OUT AND TRAVEL

The first thing to be aware of in regard to eating out is that there cannot be improvement in health if one is eating out on a frequent basis, unless one has access to a high quality health food restaurant. However, even health food restaurants are using a variety of substances that promote poor health in the individual with candida or SIBO, like cane sugar, honey, coconut sugar, whole grains, and high-carb foods. Therefore, eating out should be kept to a minimum.

When you do eat out, then it is critical to choose foods that will be less detrimental to your health. Stick with simple things like steak and steamed vegetables, eggs, or grilled chicken salad. Fresh fruit, sunflower seeds, and pumpkin seeds can be used as dessert. Even many mainstream restaurants have a gluten-free option and some places even have a paleo option. Look for lettuce wraps, low-carb, and gluten-free on the menu. If they don't have any of these options, you can ask that your burger be wrapped in lettuce instead of a bun. See the resource section at the end of this book for a website that has a database for restaurants with a paleo option.

PALEO DELIVERY

There are a variety of services that will deliver ready to eat paleo meals right to your doorstep. If you're too busy for cooking and can afford this option, this can be a real time saver. However, please be aware that many of the meals you find in these businesses may not be low enough in carb, so be sure to shop carefully and count your carbs. Of course, you'll want to rule out any that contain other ingredients you may be eliminating as well like nightshades, etc. One great way to use paleo delivery is as a supplement to your meal preparation. You could do your own cooking on a day-to-day basis, but keep some paleo meal delivery in the freezer for emergencies or special occasions. Alternatively, the delivery service could be used only a couple times a week on your busiest days or during a treatment routine when you may be too incapacitated to cook. Of course, this service is a little costly, so it won't be cost-effective for many people. You can find a list of businesses that provide paleo meal delivery in the resource section on page 198.

Paleo for Candida at a Glance

Foods to Eat Freely

animal protein (grass-fed, pastured, hormone and antibiotic free, organic, and cage-free):

beef	duck	turkey
buffalo (bison)	lamb	venison
chicken	ostrich	other wild game

low-starch vegetables

Foods to Assess and Moderate Accordingly

apple cider vinegar	eggs	nuts and seeds
avocados	fruit	olives
bone broth	high-FODMAP foods	salt (only rock salt or Himalayan salt, not table salt)
butter, ghee, heavy cream, cream cheese, hard cheese	high-glutamate foods	
	high-histamine foods	seafood
coconut	high-oxalate foods	stevia
	nightshades	

Occasional Paleo-Friendly Indulgences

beets	parsnips	tomato sauce
cassava	plantains	winter squash (e.g., butternut, acorn)
chestnuts	sweet potato	
dried fruit	tapioca	yam
lotus root	taro	

Occasional Non-Paleo Indulgences

buckwheat	quinoa	wild rice
carob	soft cheese	yogurt
potato		

Foods to Avoid Completely

agave	artificial sweeteners (acesulfame potassium, aspartame, sucralose, and others that might enter the market)	legumes
alcohol		maple syrup
all forms of sugar (including fructose, white sugar, powdered sugar, brown sugar, date sugar, beet sugar, organic sugar, organic cane juice, organic cane syrup, coconut sugar, coconut nectar)		microwaved foods
		molasses
	barley malt	refined grains
	chocolate	refined/processed foods
	coffee	
	fruit juice	rice syrup
	high-fructose corn syrup	soda pop
	honey	tea (black and green)
		whole grains

In general, your Paleo for Candida plate should be composed of animal protein, fat, and low-starch vegetables, in that order (including your snacks). Unless you prefer keto, then it would be fat, animal protein, and carb. It should always be low-carb.

Sample Meal Plans

All meals can be found in the recipe section further ahead. All food used in your meal plans should be organic, grass-fed, cage-free, hormone- and antibiotic-free.

SAMPLE MEAL PLAN • WEEK ONE

▨ MONDAY

Breakfast—Beef minute steaks with peppers and cinnamon cabbage.

Lunch—Basic bunless beef burger with lettuce, tomato, and/or avocado.

Dinner—Ground beef with left over cinnamon cabbage.

*****Dessert**—Cinnamon baked pears with pecans.

Snack—Leftover minute steak or hamburger.

▨ TUESDAY

Breakfast—Salmon patties with steamed cauliflower in butter, ghee, or preferred oil.

Lunch—Chicken tenders and mock mashed potatoes.

Dinner—Turn leftover chicken tenders into chicken salad supreme.

*****Dessert**—Mixed berries and nuts.

Snack—Chicken tenders or piece of salmon.

▓ WEDNESDAY

Breakfast—Crustless quiche with sausage and veggies.

Lunch—Baked turkey breast and broccoli soup.

Dinner—Leftover turkey breast cubed and put into leftover broccoli soup.

*Dessert—Spiced peaches and cream paradise.

Snack—Piece of sausage or sliced turkey.

▓ THURSDAY

Breakfast—Buffalo steak and fried eggs with sautéed spinach.

Lunch—Buffalo steak stir fry with refreshing cucumber and avocado salad.

Dinner—Simple buffalo roast with veggies.

*Dessert—Strawberries and cream.

Snack—Steak slices with a piece of avocado.

▓ FRIDAY

Breakfast—Leftover buffalo roast with celery and carrots.

Lunch—Caveman's palate meat loaf with garlic flavored Brussels sprouts.

Dinner—Leftover lunch.

*Dessert—Banana cream bites.

Snack—Piece of buffalo roast or meat loaf.

---

*Dessert should not be eaten on a daily basis, especially in the early phases of recovery, or in any other phase, if it produces significant symptoms or cravings for sugar and carbs. As demonstrated above, snacks should consist of animal protein and fat.

▨ SATURDAY

Breakfast—Zucchini noodle and chicken sausage casserole.

Lunch—Leftover breakfast.

Dinner—Mustard and herb chicken thighs with cauliflower rice.

*Dessert—Cherries drizzled in almond butter.

Snack—Piece of sausage or chicken thigh.

▨ SUNDAY

Breakfast—Lamb chops and celery soup.

Lunch—Lamb burgers and leftover soup.

Dinner—Mexican Paleo wrap.

*Dessert—Simply sautéed fruit with nuts.

Snack—Lamb chop or burger.

SAMPLE MEAL PLAN • WEEK TWO

▨ MONDAY

Breakfast—Lemon and herb chicken with cauliflower rice.

Lunch—Leftover chicken breasts with California blend vegetables.

Dinner—Chicken salad medley.

*Dessert—Raspberry cobbler.

Snack—Cubed chicken pieces.

▨ TUESDAY

Breakfast—Quick and simple paleo omelet with vegetables.

Lunch—Simple beef roast with veggies.

Dinner—Beef and veggie wraps.

*Dessert—Peach crumble.

Snack—Slice of roast or piece of omelet.

WEDNESDAY

Breakfast—Southwestern turkey burger.

Lunch—Turkey loaf and roasted broccoli.

Dinner—Leftover turkey loaf and mock mashed potatoes.

*Dessert—Sunflower macaroons.

Snack—Turkey burger or piece of turkey loaf.

THURSDAY

Breakfast—Crock pot stew with bison meat.

Lunch—Leftover stew.

Dinner—All the fixins bison burger.

*Dessert—Celery with macadamia butter.

Snack—Piece of stew meat, leftover burger.

FRIDAY

Breakfast—Baked salmon fillets in lemon and garlic with pepper and spinach egg scramble.

Lunch—Broiled chicken breast and zucchini noodles in butter or ghee.

Dinner—Shredded chicken breast put in zucchini soup.

*Dessert—Banana dipped in sunflower butter.

Snack—Sliced chicken breast or piece of salmon fillet.

---

*Dessert should not be eaten on a daily basis, especially in the early phases of recovery, or in any other phase, if it produces significant symptoms or cravings for sugar and carbs. As demonstrated above, snacks should consist of animal protein and fat.

SATURDAY

Breakfast—Hard boiled egg and avocado sandwich.

Lunch—Ground beef and stir fried cabbage.

Dinner—Beef stuffed cabbage rolls.

*Dessert—Macadamia cremes.

Snack—Hard boiled egg or cabbage roll.

SUNDAY

Breakfast—Leftover stuffed cabbage rolls.

Lunch—Shepherd's pie.

Dinner—Leftover Shepherd's pie

*Dessert—Cinnamon baked apple.

Snack—Beef jerky.

BEVERAGES

The following beverages may be consumed throughout the day. Every day.

- Water
- Sparkling mineral water
- Sparkling mineral water with a dash of lemon or lime
- Herbal tea (no caffeinated teas)

---

*Dessert should not be eaten on a daily basis, especially in the early phases of recovery, or in any other phase, if it produces significant symptoms or cravings for sugar and carbs. As demonstrated above, snacks should consist of animal protein and fat.

MAIN COURSE MEALS

Basic Roasted Turkey Breast

INGREDIENTS

3 lbs turkey breast (boneless and skinless if you have glutamate issues)

½ stick of butter, ghee, or coconut oil

2 tablespoons water

Salt and pepper to taste

Instructions

1. Put breast in baking dish with water in the bottom.

2. Rub it with butter and sprinkle with salt and pepper.

3. Preheat oven to 350.

4. Bake until a meat thermometer inserted into the thickest part of the breast reads 160 degrees and allow the turkey breast to rest for at least 5 minutes before slicing (about an hour).

Options

- Could sprinkle with any herbs you like before baking. Dried thyme or rosemary work splendidly.

- Good served with broccoli soup, zucchini soup, garlic flavored Brussels sprouts, roasted zucchini, mock mashed potatoes, all of which are found in this book, or any preferred vegetable.

Baked Chicken Tenders

METHOD ONE

INGREDIENTS

2 lbs of chicken tenders

1 cup of melted butter,
ghee, or coconut oil

Salt and coarse ground
pepper to taste

Parsley to taste

Instructions

1. Preheat oven to 350.

2. Put melted butter in bowl.

3. Line baking dish with parchment paper.

4. Dip chicken tenders in butter and stick them in baking dish in a single layer.

5. Sprinkle each one with salt, pepper, and parsley. Turn and sprinkle other side.

6. Bake for about 30 minutes.

METHOD TWO

INGREDIENTS

2 lbs of chicken tenders

1 cup of melted butter,
ghee or coconut oil

½ cup coconut flour

Salt and coarse ground
pepper to taste

Parsley to taste

Instructions

1. Preheat oven to 425.

2. Put the melted butter in a bowl.

3. Mix the coconut flour and spices together in a separate bowl.

4. Dip each chicken tender into the butter and then into the flour mixture. Coat both sides.

5. Place the chicken tenders in the baking dish in a single layer.

6. Could dip and coat twice if want extra coating.

7. Bake at 425 for about 20 minutes.

Options for Either Method

- Could add other spices like oregano, basil, cayenne, sage, thyme, or garlic.

- Makes a great main dish or snack.

- Could serve with Cynthia's barbecue sauce on page 132, in a salad, with mock mashed potatoes, cauliflower rice, or pretty much any other vegetable.

- Bake a big batch so you can stick some in the freezer to keep for snacking or an emergency meal.

▰ Fresh Chicken Salad Medley ▰

INGREDIENTS

6 to 8 oz cooked chicken breast (skinless) cut into cubes

½ cup steamed green beans chopped into half-inch pieces

2 tbsp sliced olives

2 tbsp chopped onion

½ tsp chopped garlic

2 tbsp olive oil

1 tbsp lemon juice

Sprinkle of crushed red pepper

Salt and pepper to taste

Instructions

1. Mix everything together in a bowl and chill before serving.

Options

- Could use apple cider vinegar for a treat once in a while.

- Olive oil could be replaced with other preferred oil.

- Additional herbs, vegetables, or spices could be added or used as substitutions.

Pasta-Free Spaghetti in Meat Sauce

INGREDIENTS

1 lb of ground beef or buffalo

1 jar of chunky organic spaghetti sauce with onion and garlic

1 spaghetti squash

Sprig of parsley

Stevia to taste

Instructions

1. Place the spaghetti squash in a dish and bake at 375 for an hour.

2. While the squash is baking, place the ground beef in a skillet and brown, draining off fat as it renders.

3. Pour the spaghetti sauce in with the ground beef and let it simmer until squash is ready. Add stevia to desired sweetness, or omit if you don't want it sweet.

4. When the squash is done, take it out of the oven and it cut it in half horizontally, not length wise.

5. Scoop out the seeds and stuff in the middle and set aside. (Seeds can be roasted and eaten just like pumpkin seeds and are a good low-carb food as well.)

6. Take a fork and scrape across the flesh of the squash. It will break apart and look like spaghetti.

7. Place desired amount of squash on your plate and top it with the meat sauce.

8. Garnish with a sprig of parsley.

Options

- You could use steamed cabbage instead of spaghetti squash. Just cut a head of cabbage into slices lengthwise and steam them and serve the meat sauce on top of them.

- Zucchini or yellow squash and California blend vegetables (broccoli, cauliflower, and carrots) also taste great with spaghetti sauce and make a fantastic pasta replacement. Zucchini and yellow squash can also be made into noodles, as described on page 114.

- Meatballs on page 102 could be used instead of meat sauce.

Avocado and Hard-Boiled Egg Sandwich

INGREDIENTS

3 hard boiled eggs

½ avocado

Salt and pepper to taste

Preferred spices to taste

Instructions

1. Slice the eggs and avocado into pieces horizontally.

2. Place half the egg slices on a plate and then place a slice of avocado on top of each egg slice.

3. Then top the avocado with the another slice of egg.

4. Sprinkle with salt, pepper, and spices you prefer.

5. Spices that work well here are turmeric, garlic powder, onion powder, chili pepper, and paprika.

Options

- Could put a slice of olive, cucumber and/or onion in between the egg halves as well.

- This could be a nice breakfast, lunch, or dinner or it can be used as a snack in the early phases of the diet when a snack is needed between meals.

Meatza Pizza Pie

CRUST INGREDIENTS

1 lb ground beef

1 egg

Seasoning of choice (basil, oregano, or onion powder are good)

1 garlic clove minced

Salt and pepper

TOPPING INGREDIENTS

1 tbsp coconut oil, butter, or ghee

½ chopped red onion

½ cup mixed bell pepper (red, yellow, and green) chopped

½ cup sliced black olives

1 zucchini sliced into ½ inch rounds

½ tsp basil

½ tsp oregano

1 8 oz. can of tomato paste, thinned out with just enough water to make it spreadable

Salt and pepper to taste

Instructions

1. Preheat oven to 350.

2. Put meat, egg, and crust spices in a bowl.

3. Mix together well and shape into a ball.

4. Place it on a baking sheet that has a rim.

5. Form into the shape of a pizza crust on the baking sheet with your hands.

6. Bake for about 15 minutes or until it is done as you prefer.

7. While it is baking, put onion, zucchini, and peppers in coconut oil and stir fry until tender.

8. Put tomato paste in a bowl and add salt, pepper, oregano and basil.

9. Spread the paste sauce over the meat crust in the same manner as a regular crust.

10. Top with onion, peppers, zucchini, and olive.

11. Put it back in the oven for another 5 or 10 minutes.

12. Remove from the oven and let it cool for a few minutes. Slice into pizza-size pieces.

13. Serve with salad, steamed kale, or sautéed spinach.

14. Eat leftovers for breakfast or lunch the next day.

Options

- You can omit the tomato sauce if you're avoiding nightshades and use different toppings like broccoli, spinach, or kale.

- If you're avoiding eggs, you could use a tablespoon or two of coconut flour instead of egg to help hold it together.

- You could use ground lamb instead of beef or bison if you wanted more of a Greek style pizza, adding more black olives, a small sprinkle of feta cheese, and extra oregano to complete the effect.

- Grated cheese could be sprinkled on top.

- Sun dried tomatoes or artichoke hearts could be included.

Mustard and Herb Chicken Thighs

INGREDIENTS

1½ lbs of chicken thighs (skinless and boneless)

½ tsp sage

½ tsp dry mustard

½ tsp garlic powder

¼ to ½ cup butter, ghee, or coconut oil (melted)

Salt and pepper to taste

2 tbsp chives, minced

Instructions

1. Place chicken thighs in a glass baking dish.

2. Mix all the other ingredients together, except for the chives.

3. Pour the mixture over the thighs and toss them a bit to coat them thoroughly.

4. Bake at 350 for one hour. Allow to rest and then top with the minced chives.

Basic Bunless Burger

INGREDIENTS

1 lb of ground beef, bison, lamb, or turkey

Salt and pepper to taste

8 lettuce leaves

Instructions

1. Make four burgers out of the ground meat.

2. Season with salt and pepper to taste.

3. Cook in broiler until done as preferred.

4. Place burger between lettuce leaves, as if they were two sides of a bun.

Options

- Add $1/2$ cup minced onion to meat mixture.

- Slice of onion.

- Slice of tomato.

- Slice of cheese.

- Slice of avocado.

- Add dry mustard to the burger mixture.

- Any herb or spice of your choice.

- Steamed cabbage leaves could be used instead of lettuce.

Shepherd's Pie

INGREDIENTS

FOR FILLING

1 lb ground beef or bison (or sausage)

3 celery stalks cut into medium dice

2 carrots cut into a medium dice

½ onion cut into medium diced

Salt and pepper to taste

½ tsp paprika

½ tsp cinnamon

FOR TOPPING

1 head of cauliflower

2 tbsp of butter, ghee, or coconut oil

Salt and pepper to taste

1 tsp dry mustard

Instructions

1. Preheat oven to 350.

2. Steam cauliflower until tender.

3. When done, pour out the water, remove steamer, and place cauliflower in the pan.

4. Add the ghee, butter, or coconut oil, salt, pepper, and dry mustard.

5. Put it into a food processor until mixed well. Should be roughly the consistency of mashed potatoes. Set aside.

6. Sauté the ground beef or sausage with the celery, carrots, onion, and salt and pepper in a skillet.

7. Drain excess fat.

8. Place the ground beef mixture in a casserole baking dish.

9. Season with salt, pepper, and paprika.

10. Put cauliflower mixture on top of the meat mixture.

11. Bake for about 30 minutes. The cauliflower on top should begin to brown. If it doesn't, you can place the entire dish under the broiler for about a minute.

Options

- Could use ground buffalo or lamb instead of beef.

- Leftovers make a great breakfast or lunch for the next day.

Lemon & Herb Chicken

INGREDIENTS

4 boneless and skinless
chicken breasts

1 lemon

¼ tsp dry mustard

2 tbsp coconut oil, ghee, or butter

3 tbsp minced garlic

3 tbsp minced onion

2 tbsp chopped parsley

Salt and pepper to taste

Instructions

1. Preheat oven to 350.

2. Cut lemon in half and squeeze juice from both halves into a cup, straining out or removing seeds.

3. Add everything but parsley to the lemon juice.

4. Put chicken in a glass baking dish.

5. Coat thoroughly with oil and herb mixture.

6. Bake until chicken breast registers 160 degrees with a meat thermometer (about 60 minutes) and allow meat to rest at least 5 minutes.

7. Sprinkle with parsley and serve. Goes great with cauliflower rice, mock mashed potatoes, or cucumber and avocado salad, all found within this book.

Beef & Veggie Wraps

INGREDIENTS

6 slices of roast beef

6 slices of avocado

6 pieces iceberg lettuce

6 slices of tomato

6 slices of onion

Salt and pepper to taste

Instructions

1. Place each piece of beef on a plate flat.

2. Place a slice of avocado, piece of lettuce, slice of tomato, and slice of onion on top of each piece of beef.

3. Sprinkle with salt pepper.

4. Wrap each piece into a log and secure with a toothpick.

5. Makes a great main course meal at breakfast, lunch, or dinner or a snack at anytime. Good for picnics, traveling, and road trips.

Aromatic Roasted Pheasant with Carrots and Celery

INGREDIENTS

1 pheasant

6 carrots chopped into half-inch pieces

6 stalks of celery chopped into half-inch pieces

1 tsp thyme

1 tsp sage

2 tbsp butter or coconut oil

Salt and pepper

Instructions

1. Preheat oven to 400.

2. Sauté carrots and celery together with melted butter or coconut oil until slightly tender. Add herbs to mixture and take off heat.

3. Place pheasant in baking dish breast side up.

4. Dry the skin of the pheasant using a paper towel and then season generously with salt and pepper remembering to season the cavity as well.

5. Stuff the cavity with vegetable mixture.

6. Bake for 15 minutes.

7. Reduce heat to 350 and bake for 25 minutes per pound. Pheasant should register 160 degrees with a meat thermometer and the juices should run clear.

8. Let sit for 15 minutes before carving.

9. Pheasant is quite lean so be careful not to overcook or it will dry out. It is a little pinker in color than chicken when done.

Savory Slow-Cooked Brisket

INGREDIENTS

3 lb beef brisket

1 head of cabbage

1 onion

½ tsp of cinnamon

1 tsp crushed red pepper

2 cups beef broth

Salt and coarse ground pepper

Instructions

1. Place the brisket in baking dish.

2. Sprinkle with salt and pepper.

3. Place in oven at 425 degrees.

4. Bake it for 10 to 15 minutes or until golden brown, turning it a few times through the process.

5. Take out of the oven and put it in the slow cooker.

6. Slice cabbage into thick ribbons, taking care to remove the core.

7. Cut onion into slices. Place onion and cabbage in the cooker around the meat.

8. Mix broth and spices together and pour in cooker.

9. Cook for 6 to 8 hours.

Jalapeño and Guacamole Burger

INGREDIENTS

1 lb of ground beef or bison

1 or 2 jalapeños (depending how spicy you want it) seeds removed and finely minced

Salt and pepper

Guacamole from page 116

Instructions

1. Quarter jalapeño and remove the seeds. Using a sharp knife, cut into a fine mince.

2. Break up ground beef or bison in a bowl.

3. Add salt, pepper, and jalapeño.

4. Cook in broiler until done.

5. Top with guacamole.

Options

• Could wrap burger in a piece of lettuce or steamed cabbage leaf after it is done if desired.

INGREDIENTS

1 lb salmon filet	¼ cup parsley and/or dill
1 tsp onion powder	1 tbsp lemon juice
1 egg	Salt and pepper
2 tbsp coconut flour	

Instructions

1. Cut the salmon filet into medium cubes and put in your food processor with all other ingredients. Process until it has a smooth texture and the mix is homogenous.

2. Scrape salmon into a bowl using a spatula.

3. Form into four tightly packed patties.

4. Broil for 7 minutes on one side then turn over and broil for another 7 minutes.

Options

• Top with romaine lettuce, tomato, and/or avocado.

• Good served with cauliflower rice, cinnamon cabbage, sautéed spinach, or any of the soups (broccoli, cauliflower, celery, or zucchini), all found in this book.

Southwestern Turkey Burger

INGREDIENTS

1 lb ground turkey

2 tbsp coconut flour

½ chopped onion

1 minced garlic

1 tsp cumin

1 egg

Guacamole from page 116

Lettuce and tomato slices

Instructions

1. Put ground turkey in a bowl.

2. Add all ingredients except guacamole, lettuce, and tomato. Mix thoroughly and form into four patties.

3. Cook in broiler until done.

4. Top with guacamole, lettuce, and tomato.

Options

1. Could add sun dried tomatoes and/or bell peppers to turkey mixture before cooking.

Simple Roast Duck

INGREDIENTS

1 whole duck, 4–6 lbs

Salt and pepper to taste

Preferred spices (e.g. paprika, pepper, onion powder, garlic powder)

Instructions

1. Remove giblets.

2. Rinse off the duck inside and out and pat dry with paper towel.

3. Score skin with knife or poke with a toothpick. Slice skin only, being careful not to cut into meat.

4. Preheat oven to 350.

5. Place in a dish breast side up.

6. Fold neck skin under.

7. Sprinkle with salt and pepper.

8. Rub spices on skin.

9. Place in a Dutch oven with a rack on bottom. Duck has a lot of fat, you want to keep it out of the fat while cooking.

10. Baste the duck every half hour with juices in bottom of pan.

11. Cook 1 hour and 45 minutes.

12. Turn up to 425 and bake 15 more minutes or until golden brown. A meat thermometer inserted into the thickest part of the thigh should register 155 degrees.

13. Fat can be saved in fridge for frying.

14. Let it sit for about 15 minutes before serving.

15. Goes well served with garlic roasted Brussels sprouts, mock mashed potatoes, or baked asparagus, all found in this book.

Crock Pot Stew

INGREDIENTS

1½ lbs of stew meat
(any cut of chuck)

4 carrots

1 onion

4 stalks of celery

1 cup cut green beans

½ tsp garlic powder

2 cups of water

Salt and pepper to taste

Instructions

1. Cut vegetables into 1 inch by 1 inch.

2. Add everything to the crock pot. Adjust until water nearly covers the meat (to about ¾ the height of the meat).

3. Cook 6 to 8 hours.

Seared Duck Breast

INGREDIENTS

2 duck breasts

Salt and pepper

Instructions

1. Preheat oven to 350.
2. Thaw the breasts.
3. Pat dry with paper towel.
4. Score the skin into $1/4$ inch intervals making crisscross pattern—don't cut into flesh.
5. Season with salt and pepper.
6. Place breast skin side down into skillet.
7. Cook over low heat, draining off fat as breast renders.
8. Turn over when skin side is golden brown and cook 1 to 2 minutes on the other side.
9. Place in oven for 5 to 6 minutes.
10. Let it rest for 10 minutes before serving.

Options

- Could add different spices, if you prefer, like allspice or cinnamon.
- Serve with cinnamon cabbage, roasted broccoli, zucchini or yellow squash, or garlic flavored Brussels sprouts, all found in this book.

All the Fixins Bison Burger

INGREDIENTS

1 lb ground bison

1 tbsp minced garlic

$1/4$ cup chopped onion

1 avocado sliced

1 tomato sliced

4 lettuce leaves

Salt and pepper

Instructions

1. Mix bison, garlic, onion, salt, and pepper in a bowl.

2. Form into four burgers.

3. Cook on broiler until done.

4. Place on plate and top with lettuce, tomato, and avocado.

Options

● Could use beef instead of bison.

● A slice of cheese could be included.

Simple Steak Salad

INGREDIENTS

1 cooked steak cut into bite size pieces

Basic dressing from page 121

Bowl of salad with the following:

Romaine lettuce

Tomato

Onion

Cucumbers

Olives

Avocado

Lightly toasted pumpkin seeds

Instructions

1. To toast pumpkin seed, place seeds on a sheet tray. Drizzle with coconut oil and cook for 5 minutes at 300 degrees or until seeds are fragrant.

2. Toss all ingredients together in a bowl.

3. Sprinkle with basic dressing. Alternatively, could use oil of your choice and apple cider vinegar if that is tolerable for you.

Options

● Could use chicken tenders or cubed chicken breast instead of steak and add any other herb or vegetable you like.

Spicy Green Beans and Ground Beef

INGREDIENTS

1 lb of ground beef

½ lb of cut green beans

2 tbsp oil of your choice
(I prefer walnut or avocado,
but olive oil is a nice change)

½ cup chopped onion
or green onion

1 tsp red pepper

2 crushed garlic cloves

Salt and pepper to taste

Instructions

1. Render ground beef in skillet over medium-high heat. After meat has browned, add in onion and cook until onion is softened.

2. Steam the green beans.

3. Mix everything together in a bowl and sprinkle with oil and remaining spices.

Options

• This recipe can be done with ground bison instead of beef.

• You could add other spices if desired, or sprinkle with a little cheese on occasion for a treat.

Broiled Hot Dogs with Fried Cabbage

INGREDIENTS

1 head of cabbage

1 package of organic beef hot
dogs (sugar-free and nitrate-
free—see resource section)

¼ tsp dry mustard

Salt and pepper

Instructions

1. Steam cabbage. Then stir fry it in a skillet for a few minutes with water or a little coconut oil or butter.

2. Broil hot dogs until begin to brown a bit.

3. Slice the hot dogs into little pieces and mix with the cabbage, dry mustard, salt, and pepper.

4. It's important that you use organic hot dogs. Traditional hot dogs from the mainstream grocery store contain all kinds of unhealthy ingredients and should not be eaten. See resource section.

Ground Beef or Bison with Stir Fried Cabbage

INGREDIENTS

1 lb of ground bison or beef	1 avocado
1 head of cabbage	½ cup chopped onion or green onion
1 tbsp of coconut oil or butter or water	Salt and pepper to taste

Instructions

1. Cook ground beef or bison in skillet.

2. Steam the cabbage and then stir fry it lightly in coconut oil, butter, or water.

3. Then mix cabbage and cooked beef together.

4. Add salt, pepper, and onion.

5. Top with avocado slices.

Options

• Could include chopped garlic and/or olives.

Pepper and Spinach Egg Scramble

INGREDIENTS

2 or 3 eggs

½ cup or so of chopped green, yellow, and red peppers (I like Woodstock Organics frozen)

A little butter, ghee, or coconut oil

½ cup of chopped spinach

Salt and pepper to taste

Instructions

1. Stir fry the peppers with the butter, ghee, or oil in a skillet until tender.

2. Add spinach to peppers for a couple minutes. Drain off any extra water and set aside.

3. Scramble eggs in bowl.

4. Add eggs to a medium-high skillet and stir frequently until eggs are scrambled to desired doneness.

5. Add spinach and peppers.

6. Season with salt and pepper.

Options

- Top with guacamole from page 116.
- Add onion and garlic powder.
- Sometimes I like to buy Applegate Farms sliced turkey bologna, cut it into pieces, and throw it in with the eggs too.
- You could also add pieces of sausage.
- Cheese could be sprinkled on top of it as a treat once in a while.

Caveman's Palate Meat Loaf

INGREDIENTS

½ cup of chopped onion

½ tsp of organic garlic powder

½ tsp salt

½ tsp pepper

5 oz mixed bell peppers—
green, yellow, and red
(see resource section)

½ cup of chopped spinach

½ tsp dry mustard

1 tbsp organic coconut flour

2 eggs

2 lbs ground beef

1 6 oz can of organic tomato paste,
thin out slightly with water so
that tomato paste has roughly
the consistency of ketchup

Instructions

1. Preheat oven to 350.

2. Break up the ground beef in a large bowl.

3. Sweat peppers in a small skillet over medium heat with coconut oil until soft and sweet. Add to bowl.

4. Add all the ingredients except for the tomato paste.

5. Mix together thoroughly. If possible use a mixer with a paddle attachment.

6. Stick in a baking dish and form into a loaf.

7. Bake for 40 minutes, then pull it out and cover it with tomato paste.

8. Bake for another 10 or 15 minutes.

Options

- I like to have leftovers for the next day or to put in the freezer, so I used 2 pounds of meat. You could use 1 pound if you like and cut other ingredients in half.

- You could also feel free to add any other kind of spice or condiment you desire.

- This easy and flavorful recipe makes a great entree any time of day — breakfast, lunch, or dinner. It's so moist, firm, and delicious, and it is a breeze to throw together.

- Can eat by itself since it is filled with vegetables or serve with any of the soups or sides provided in this book, like cauliflower rice or cucumber and avocado salad.

Turkey Loaf

INGREDIENTS

1½ lb of ground turkey

½ cup chopped spinach

½ cup chopped celery

1 egg

½ medium onion chopped

½ tsp sage powder

Sliced olives

Salt and pepper to taste

Instructions

1. Preheat oven to 375.

2. Put ground turkey in a bowl.

3. Sweat onion and celery over medium-low heat with a little water or coconut oil. When vegetables are softened, add spinach in skillet until slightly tender.

4. Add them to turkey.

5. Add egg, salt, sage, and pepper.

6. Mix well.

7. Form into a loaf in a baking dish.

8. Bake 50 or 60 minutes. When a toothpick inserted into the thickest part of the meatloaf comes out clean it is finished.

9. Take out of oven and top with sliced olives.

10. Can be eaten alone since it is already rich in vegetables or goes well with zucchini soup, celery soup, or cauliflower rice also found in this book.

Holiday Kraut & Dogs Casserole

INGREDIENTS

1 jar organic sauerkraut

½ tsp dry mustard

Salt and pepper to taste

1 package of organic, sugar-free, and nitrate-free hot dogs (see resource section)

Instructions

1. Put the sauerkraut in a bowl and toss with dry mustard and salt and pepper as desired.

2. Pour half the sauerkraut in a glass dish.

3. Place hot dogs on top of sauerkraut.

4. Pour the remaining sauerkraut on top of the hot dogs.

5. Cover with a lid.

6. Bake at 350 for about 40 minutes.

7. Can be served with mock mashed potatoes on page 127.

Options

● Could use sausage instead of hot dogs.

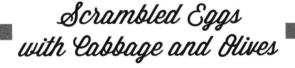

Scrambled Eggs with Cabbage and Olives

INGREDIENTS

½ cup of chopped and steamed cabbage

2 or 3 eggs

2 tbsp of sliced olives

Butter, ghee, or coconut oil

Pepper

Instructions

1. Steam cabbage. Then stir fry briefly in oil, butter, or ghee.

2. Add eggs and olives and scramble together.

3. Sprinkle with pepper.

Options

● I like this without salt, but you can add salt if desired.

● Could add other herbs and spices if you like.

Simple Roast with Vegetables

INGREDIENTS

1 beef or buffalo roast
(I like eye of round, chuck,
or bottom round roast)

1 package of celery hearts
sliced length-wise

6 to 8 carrots sliced length-wise

1 fresh onion sliced

Salt and pepper

Approximately 1 cup of water

Instructions

1. Preheat oven to 300.

2. Line the bottom of a glass baking dish with celery, carrot, and half of the onion slices.

3. Place roast on top of vegetables.

4. Place the remaining sliced onions on top of the roast.

5. Sprinkle everything with salt and pepper.

6. Add water.

7. Cover.

8. Bake for 3 hours or until a meat thermometer inserted into the thickest part of the roast registers 145 degrees for medium.

9. Allow to rest 10 minutes. Serve with juices poured over meat and vegetables.

Easy Minute Steaks with Mixed Peppers

INGREDIENTS

1 package of beef minute steaks

1 package of mixed bell peppers
or you can cut them fresh if you
like (green, yellow, and red)
See resource section

Coconut oil or ghee

Garlic powder to taste

Onion powder to taste

Salt and pepper to taste

Instructions

1. Sauté steaks and peppers together in ghee or coconut oil until preferred doneness.

2. Sprinkle with garlic powder, onion powder, pepper, and salt.

Options

- You could add chopped onions to this if you wish and you could use any other kind of vegetable you like as well or in place of the peppers.

Baked Chicken Breast with California Blend Vegetables

INGREDIENTS

4 chicken breasts

1 16-oz bag of California blend style veggies (includes cauliflower, broccoli, carrots and sometimes zucchini)

Olive oil (could also use butter, ghee, or oil of your choice)

¼ tsp of sage

Spice of your choice (garlic and onion are good)

Salt and pepper to taste

Instructions

1. Bake chicken breasts in small baking dish with a little water, salt, and pepper in the oven until tender (350 for about an hour).

2. Steam California blend vegetables.

3. Cut chicken up into bite size pieces.

4. Toss all the ingredients together in a bowl and add olive oil, butter, or ghee, and spices and salt.

5. Can be eaten warm or cold, when made with oil. If using butter or ghee, then needs to be eaten immediately while warm.

Chicken Salad Supreme

INGREDIENTS

1 lb of cubed chicken
breast already cooked

1 head of romaine lettuce

1 tomato diced

½ onion chopped

1 avocado

½ sliced cucumber

Basic dressing on page 121,
but add garlic powder to it

Salt and pepper to taste

2 tbsp lightly toasted
pumpkin seeds

Instructions

1. Toss all ingredients together, except pumpkin seeds.

2. Pour on basic dressing.

3. Sprinkle with pumpkin seeds.

Mexican Paleo Wrap

INGREDIENTS

1 lb ground beef

½ tsp or to taste Mexican seasoning
blend (cumin, coriander, garlic,
cilantro, oregano, cayenne)

1 cup chopped tomatoes

½ cup chopped onion
or green onion

1 sliced avocado

Lettuce leaves or steamed
cabbage leaves

Salt and pepper

Instructions

1. Render ground beef in a pan over medium-high heat. When the meat is browned, drain off excess fat and add spices.

2. Spread across a leaf of lettuce or a steamed cabbage leaf.

3. Top with tomatoes, onion and avocado.

4. Wrap similar to a burrito and eat.

◾ Options

- Could add shredded cheese once in a while as a treat.

- Bison could be used instead of beef.

- Guacamole from page 116 could replace the sliced avocado.

Hoagie-less Sausage with Peppers and Onions

INGREDIENTS

1 package of preservative-free, nitrate-free, sugar-free, Italian sausage (see resource section)

1 package of mixed bell peppers or you can cut them fresh too if you like (see resource section)

1 onion sliced

Water

◾ Instructions

1. Combine sausage, peppers, and onion in a glass dish.

2. Cover with a little water and a lid.

3. Bake for about 40 minutes at 350.

◾ Options

- If you can't do peppers or onions, they could be replaced with spinach, cabbage, broccoli, or cauliflower.

- Sausage could be beef, bison, turkey, or chicken.

- Serve with your favorite organic tomato sauce.

Fast and Easy Paleo Pizza

I was worried that the end product of the Paleo Pizza would not live up to the delicious fantasy I had in my head, but it actually exceeded my expectations. Honestly, I felt this was as rich and tasty as any pizza I've ever had in my non-paleo days, without the guilt or negative effects on physical or emotional health. This recipe was originally inspired by a recipe I found at the Paleo Bread™ website, but I made several changes to it.

INGREDIENTS

4 slices of coconut Paleo Bread™ (see resource section)

4 tbsp organic tomato paste

1 cup of sliced green, yellow, and red peppers

4 Italian beef sausage links (see resource section)

A few shakes of basil and oregano

1 clove chopped garlic

A dash of salt and pepper

½ cup chopped onion

1 tsp of coconut oil

¼ cup sliced olives

1 cup of shredded cheese (optional)

Instructions

1. Cook the sausage in a skillet. Cover with a lid to keep warm when done.

2. Sweat the peppers with onion and garlic until tender in the coconut oil.

3. Shred the cheese and sit to the side.

4. Toast the bread lightly in the toaster.

5. Spread 1 tablespoon of tomato paste on each piece of toast.

6. Cut up the beef sausage into little pieces.

7. Sprinkle sausage on top of the toast.

8. Cover with peppers, onions, garlic, and olives.

9. Top it off with the cheese if you like or leave as is.

10. Put in the toaster oven for just a few minutes, until the cheese melts.

Options

- The coconut bread has a nice soft, chewy texture that is perfect for pizza. If you wanted a more crispy paleo pizza crust, then you could toast the bread longer.
- Beef sausage could be replaced with turkey, chicken, or bison sausage.

Pan-Roasted Lamb Chops with Herbs

INGREDIENTS

6 lamb chops	Sprinkle of garlic powder
2 tbsp coconut oil, butter, or ghee	Sprinkle of onion powder
Sprinkle of rosemary	Sprinkle of cilantro
Sprinkle of oregano	Salt and pepper to taste

Instructions

1. Preheat oven to 350.
2. Melt butter, coconut oil, or ghee in skillet over medium-high heat.
3. Put lamb chops in the skillet.
4. Brown both sides of the lamb chops for about 3 minutes each side.
5. Place your lamb chops in a glass baking dish with a touch of water.
6. Sprinkle them with salt, pepper, and herbs you desire.
7. Bake for about 10 to 15 minutes.
8. Turn them over.
9. Bake for another 10 to 15 minutes. For medium chops, a thermometer inserted into the middle of the chop should register 145 degrees.
10. Let them sit for about 5 minutes after removing from oven before serving.
11. The chops pair well with sides like mock mashed potatoes, cauliflower rice, cinnamon cabbage, garlic flavored Brussels sprouts, oven roasted asparagus, or roasted zucchini, all of which you can find in the side dish section of this book.

Crustless Quiche with Sausage and Veggies

INGREDIENTS

2 tbsp of coconut oil (or butter)

6 eggs

1 cup chopped spinach

½ cup chopped mixed green, red, and yellow peppers

½ medium onion or 4 tbsp onion flakes

½ tsp garlic powder

½ lb of beef, bison, turkey, or chicken sausage chopped (already cooked)

Pepper to taste

Instructions

1. Remove casing from sausage and break into pieces.

2. Preheat oven to 350.

3. Grease your dish with the coconut oil or butter.

4. Cook your sausage in a skillet until almost done.

5. Add your peppers and spinach and cook for a few minutes until peppers are tender.

6. Combine eggs and spices in a bowl and whisk them together.

7. Stir in spinach, peppers, and sausage.

8. Pour into the greased baking dish.

9. Bake for about 30 minutes until the eggs puff up and begin to pull away from the edge of the dish. Edges will be slightly brown.

10. Let it cool a little before removing from the dish or eating.

Options

- You can substitute the spinach and peppers with any other vegetable you desire like broccoli, chopped kale, or chard.

- Instead of mixing the meat and vegetables in with the eggs, you can place the meat and vegetables in the bottom of the pan and then pour the egg mixture on top.

- Cheese can be added to the recipe before baking by sprinkling it on top of the meat and vegetable mixture or sprinkle it on top of quiche when it is done. I like to sprinkle it on top afterwards.

- You can top it with olives, tomato slices, avocado slices, guacamole, or salsa if you like.

- If you'd like a crust, you could use the crust on page 174. Just place the crust in the bottom of the pan and pour the eggs into the crust before baking.

- Remember, eggs aren't just for breakfast; they make a great dish for lunch or dinner as well. Double or triple the batch and have leftovers for the next day.

Mouth Watering Barbecue Ribs

INGREDIENTS

3 lbs of boneless short ribs

Coconut oil

½ cup of water

Cynthia's barbecue sauce from page 132

Parsley

Instructions

1. Preheat oven to 300 degrees.

2. In a pan over medium-high heat, sear the short ribs in coconut oil, turning the ribs to make sure all sides are browned.

3. Place the ribs in a glass baking dish.

4. Dilute barbecue sauce with ½ cup water. Pour the barbecue sauce on top of them and turn them several times to coat the ribs with the sauce on all sides.

5. Cover with a lid, and bake for about 3 hours.

6. Meat will be tender and fall apart when you touch it with your fork when it is ready.

7. Top with parsley

8. Serve with mock mashed potatoes from page 127.

Leg of Lamb Roast with Celery

INGREDIENTS

4 lb boneless leg of lamb (don't remove the netting, it helps boneless keep its form)

2 tbsp lemon juice

2 garlic cloves minced

2 tbsp rosemary

2 tbsp parsley

1 ½ cup of water

1 or 2 bunches of celery

Coarse ground pepper to taste

Instructions

1. Let lamb sit at room temp for 30 or 60 minutes before cooking, so it will cook faster.

2. Preheat oven to 425.

3. Make little incisions across the meat, about one inch long.

4. Combine the lemon juice, garlic, rosemary, parsley, and pepper into a thick paste.

5. Rub it over the leg of lamb making sure to work it into the incisions a bit.

6. Pour the water into the bottom of a baking dish with a rack and line the bottom of the dish with all the stalks of celery.

7. Place the leg of lamb on the rack in the baking dish fat side up over top of the celery.

8. Place in oven uncovered.

9. Roast for 15 minutes at 425 in order to begin rendering some of the fat.

10. Reduce heat to 350 and bake about 90 minutes for medium rare or 120 minutes for well done. For medium rare a meat thermometer inserted into the thickest part of the leg should register 125 degrees. For well done, it should register 155 degrees. Baste periodically.

11. Remove from oven and let sit for 10 or 15 minutes before serving.

12. Serve with celery slices.

13. Sprinkle with salt, when served.

14. No salt while cooking or will dry it out.

Options

- Could use a $1/_2$ stick soft butter with the lemon juice and herb paste.

Fajita Bowl

INGREDIENTS

1 bowl of romaine lettuce

1 lb beef, bison, or chicken strips

$1/_2$ tsp or to taste Mexican Seasoning Blend (cumin, coriander, garlic, cilantro, oregano, cayenne)

2 tbsp lime juice

1 cup diced tomatoes

$1/_2$ cup chopped onion

$1/_2$ cup bell peppers

Guacamole from page 116

1 cup of cauliflower rice from page 113

Salt and pepper

Instructions

1. Cook beef in pan with bell peppers.

2. Add spices to beef.

3. Toss romaine with lime juice in large bowl.

4. Divide romaine into smaller individual bowls.

5. Place small serving of cauliflower rice on top of romaine.

6. Cover with serving of meat.

7. Top with diced tomatoes, onion, guacamole, salt, and pepper.

Options

- Could add shredded cheese once in a while as a treat.
- Could use Greek spices and olives instead of Mexican or replace with Italian spices.

Savory Paleo Meatballs

INGREDIENTS

½ cup chopped onion

½ tsp of organic garlic powder

½ tsp salt

½ tsp organic pepper

½ tsp oregano

½ tsp basil

5 oz mixed bell peppers—green, yellow, and red (see resource section)

1 tbsp organic coconut flour

2 eggs

2 lbs ground beef

1 jar of organic spaghetti sauce (optional)

Instructions

1. Preheat oven to 350.

2. Break up the ground beef in a large bowl.

3. Sweat peppers in a skillet over medium heat until soft. Add to bowl with ground beef.

4. Add all the ingredients except for the tomato sauce.

5. Mix together good. If possible use a mixer with a paddle attachment.

6. Form into meatballs.

7. Stick in a baking dish with a little coconut oil on the bottom.

8. Bake for 40 or 50 minutes. (Alternatively you could cook on the stove top in a skillet.)

9. If you want to use the spaghetti sauce, then put the meatballs in a large sauce pan with the sauce and simmer for 40 or 50 minutes instead of baking.

10. Serve over steamed cabbage, zucchini, spaghetti squash, zucchini noodles, or steamed vegetable of your choice like broccoli and cauliflower.

Beef Stuffed Cabbage Rolls

INGREDIENTS

1 head of cabbage cored	1¼ lb ground beef
½ cup chopped onion	Salt and pepper to taste

Instructions

1. Preheat oven to 350.

2. Cut the head of cabbage in half and steam it in vegetable steamer until tender.

3. Pull the leaves apart and set aside.

4. Sweat the onion in a skillet over medium heat until tender.

5. Mix the meat in a bowl with salt and pepper and then add the onion.

6. Sprinkle one quarter pound of the meat across the bottom of a baking dish with a little water.

7. Place a scoop of beef mixture in the middle of a cabbage leaf. Fold the leaf over on each side to form a log and completely encase the meat mixture within the leaf. If the leaf is too small to roll, then place one leaf onto another leaf and roll together. Repeat with remaining leaves.

8. Place the logs on top of the ground beef inside the baking dish.

9. Cover with a lid and bake for about 60 minutes.

Options

• Top with favorite organic tomato sauce.

Homemade Jerky

Jerky makes a great snack, a last minute meal, or something you can use to hold you over if hunger hits before the meal is ready. You can also take it on a plane, road trip, or hiking, or put it in a stocking or Easter Basket on the holiday. However, most of the jerky on the market is loaded with substances that you don't want to eat. Even many of the health store brands have evaporated cane juice, honey, or spices that can be problematic for people with candida. Therefore, making your own beef jerky may be something you want to learn. However, if you don't have time, see the resource section for where to get clean jerky.

INGREDIENTS

1 or 2 lbs of desired meat (beef flank, brisket, loin, sirloin, top round, turkey breast, venison)

Salt and coarse ground pepper

Instructions

1. Use lean cuts of meat to make jerky. Fat won't cure, will go rancid, and can make you sick.

2. Freeze your meat for a couple hours, if fresh, until it is partially frozen. If already frozen, then let thaw partially.

3. Trim off as much as fat as possible.

4. You want to cut the meat while it is still partially frozen, which allows the knife to move through easily.

5. Cut it into desired pieces. Short or long, or a combination of both.

6. Put the cut pieces of meat in a Ziploc baggie with salt and pepper and a little water. Shake to coat them well. Put baggie in the fridge and let them marinate in it for several hours or overnight.

7. Take the meat out of the baggie and pat dry with clean paper towel.

8. Place on the tray in a single layer in the food dehydrator. Follow dehydrator instructions until done (typically around four hours at somewhere between 125 and 160 degrees). May need to flip at the halfway point.

9. Be careful not to over dry or it will be tough or brittle. Want them dry, but still flexible to some degree.

10. Store in the fridge in an airtight container.

Options

- Since many of the herbs, spices, and marinade options that are used in the process may be problematic for some individuals (feed candida or increase glutamate and histamine levels), I only added salt and pepper. If you would like to add other spices to your jerky, then simply put together the desired combination and marinate in the ziplock baggie in the fridge for three to eight hours before putting it in the dehydrator. (Common options include coconut aminos, apple cider vinegar, garlic powder, onion powder, paprika, and cayenne.)

- The salt and pepper marinade can be omitted, if you want completely plain jerky.

- You can ask the butcher to cut the meat for you, if you want to save time and energy.

- If you don't have a dehydrator, jerky can be made in the oven, but it takes longer. (Place on a rack that sits on top of a baking sheet with temp at about 170, for about 8 hours or until dry. May need to flip at halfway point. A convection oven may take less time.)

Quick and Simple Paleo Omelet

INGREDIENTS

3 large eggs

¼ cup coconut milk

¼ cup onion diced small

⅛ cup sliced olives

3 avocado slices

1 tbsp coconut oil
(or butter or ghee)

Instructions

1. Put eggs and coconut milk in a bowl and mix together with hand whisk.

2. Melt coconut oil in skillet.

3. Pour egg mixture into skillet.

4. Add onion and olives on one side.

5. Fold egg over.

6. Flip.

7. Cook until lightly brown.

8. Put on a plate and top with avocado slices.

Options

- Could add chopped tomatoes, guacamole from page 116, chili peppers, or bell peppers.

Cornish Hen and Vegetables

INGREDIENTS

2 cornish hens

6 carrots

6 stalks of celery

½ cup chestnuts

1 sliced onion

½ stick of butter
(or ghee or coconut oil)

1 cup of water

Salt and coarse
ground pepper

Instructions

1. Preheat the oven to 350.

2. Let the hens sit at room temperature for 30 minutes prior to cooking.

3. Coat the hens with butter, ghee, or coconut oil.

4. Sprinkle with salt and coarse ground pepper inside and out.

5. Cut the celery, carrots, and chestnuts in half.

6. Spread the carrots, onion, celery, and chestnuts across the bottom of a roasting pan in a cup of water and sprinkle with salt and pepper.

7. Sit the hens on top of the vegetables, breast side up.

8. Roast uncovered, basting periodically, until skin turns golden brown. Check after 60 minutes, hens are done when a meat thermometer inserted into the thickest part of the thigh registers 160 degrees.

Options

- Could sprinkle garlic, rosemary, thyme, sage, lemon juice or any desired herbs on hens and inside cavity to spice it up a bit.

Pasta-Free Lasagna

This is not a true Paleo for Candida recipe because it includes mozzarella cheese, which I don't typically recommend consuming. However, since eating a Paleo for Candida Diet is for life, I think some type of lasagna is just one of those things that we may want to indulge in once in a great while. This recipe gets rid of the worst offender (pasta) and if you eat a little mozzarella once or twice a year or so, there is no serious harm done, in most cases. And by using cabbage, you have a pasta-free version of lasagna that is just as delicious as it counterpart, but much healthier.

INGREDIENTS

1 head of cabbage

1 lb of ground beef or bison

1 (24 or 25) oz jar of spaghetti sauce (you could make your own, but I'm just not that much of a Betty Crocker)

1 16 oz package of mozzarella cheese

1 egg

Dash of stevia to taste

Dash of cinnamon, fennel, and/or red pepper

Instructions

1. Preheat oven to 350.

2. Brown the meat in a skillet.

3. Pour the spaghetti sauce into the meat, add stevia and spices, and simmer for about 10 minutes.

4. Remove from heat and set aside.

5. Core and cut the head of cabbage in half and place it in a vegetable steamer.

6. Steam until slightly tender or desired texture.

7. Pull the leaves apart and set aside.

8. Shred the cheese and put it in a bowl.

9. Put egg in a separate bowl and whisk. Then pour it into the meat and sauce mixture after it has cooled and stir well.

10. Place a thin layer of meat sauce in the bottom of a baking dish.

11. Cover with a layer of cabbage leaves, as if they are noodles.

12. Put a layer of meat sauce over the cabbage leaves.

13. Add a layer of cheese.

14. Cover with another layer of cabbage leaves.

15. Another layer of meat sauce.

16. Cover with cheese.

17. Bake in the oven uncovered for about 30 minutes.

18. Take out of the oven and let cool for 10 minutes before serving.

Options

- You can use the cinnamon, fennel, and red pepper together or just one or two of them in any combination. You could also omit all three of these spices, if you like. All these options taste great. Each spice gives it a slightly different flair.

- Egg can be omitted, but I include to help it hold its shape better.

- Since cabbage is a primary ingredient, this is a complete meal in and of itself, no side dish is really needed. However, it could be served with a salad.

- If you must have garlic bread as well, you could use the coconut version of Paleo Bread™ and toast it in a toaster oven with butter, salt, and garlic powder. (See the resource section on page 196 for where to find Paleo Bread.)

- This is a great lower carb dish for holidays like Easter, Christmas, or New Year's. Can also be a special treat on birthdays, anniversaries, or dinner parties.

Zucchini Noodle and Sausage Casserole

INGREDIENTS

5 zucchini

1 lb of sausage

1 cup diced tomatoes

½ onion chopped

1 clove of minced garlic

1 cup diced red bell peppers

Salt and pepper to taste

Instructions

1. Make zucchini noodles as instructed on page 114.

2. Place them in a baking dish with all the other ingredients and mix together.

3. Bake for 35 minutes uncovered.

4. Remove from oven and let sit for 10 minutes before serving.

Options

- Could add cheese for a special treat now and then.

- Mushrooms, eggplant, or other desired vegetables could be added.

- Sausage can be beef, turkey, chicken, or bison.

Baked Salmon in Lemon and Garlic Butter

INGREDIENTS

3 tbsp of lemon juice

½ tsp garlic powder

¼ tsp of pepper

¼ tsp of thyme

2 tbsp of melted butter, ghee, or coconut oil

2 5 oz salmon fillets

Instructions

1. Preheat oven to 400.

2. Mix all the ingredients together except salmon.

3. Pour mixture in baking dish.

4. Place the salmon in the mixture and turn it several times to coat it well with the mixture.

5. Let it marinate for about 15 minutes.

6. Put baking dish in oven and bake uncovered.

7. Generally, salmon fillet is baked for about 10 to 12 minutes per inch of thickness.

8. Salmon is done when it flakes easily with your fork and is opaque in color with pink lines.

9. Don't overcook or it will be dry.

10. Sprinkle with salt and pepper and serve.

11. Goes well with sautéed spinach, zucchini noodles, cabbage in olive oil, herbed kale salad, cinnamon cabbage, or any of the soups in the sides and sauces section of this book.

Bison and Cucumber Salad

INGREDIENTS

1 lb of stir fry bison

1 or 2 cucumbers

Oil of your choice (olive, walnut, sesame, macadamia, high-oleic sunflower)

½ cup chopped tomatoes

½ red onion chopped

Salt and pepper to taste

INSTRUCTIONS

1. Slice and dice cucumbers into cubes and put them in a bowl with the tomatoes and the onions.

2. Add stir fried bison meat.

3. Mix them together.

4. Sprinkle with oil of your choice, pepper, and salt.

5. Chill and serve.

OPTIONS

• Could add other things as well, like cheese, cilantro, garlic, cherry tomatoes cut in half, or anything you like.

• This is a good meal on a hot summer's day.

• You can use beef instead of bison if desired and add any other vegetable of your choice.

SIDE DISHES, SOUPS, AND SAUCES

Cauliflower Rice

INGREDIENTS

1 head of cauliflower

1 tsp of butter

Salt and pepper
to taste

Instructions

1. Break up the head of cauliflower and stick it in a food processor until it looks like rice or couscous. (This could also be done by hand with a food grater.)

2. That's all there is to it. Don't cook it until you're ready to eat. It can be made in large batches and frozen for later use if desired.

3. To cook, put cauliflower in a pan over medium-high heat with $1/4$ cup water. When nearly all water has evaporated, take off heat and stir in butter. Stir until butter is emulsified into the cauliflower. Season with salt and pepper.

4. Serve with meat and vegetables just as you would with rice.

Options

- You can add any preferred spice combination to make a Mexican, Thai, Greek, Italian, etc. dish.
- Chopped onion could be included in the sauté.
- Can be used to replace rice in any rice dish.

Zucchini Noodles

Zucchini noodles can be made in a variety of different ways. You can buy fancy gadgets, if you enjoy that kind of thing. For me, that is all too complicated and time consuming. A true spiral vegetable cutter takes up a lot of space, has to be put together and torn apart, and you might cut yourself on the very sharp blade. So, I think the easiest method is to just use your potato peeler. You could even just take a knife and cut them lengthwise in strips.

INGREDIENTS

6 small zucchini

1 tbsp coconut oil

Salt and pepper to taste

Instructions

1. Peel the skin off the zucchini and toss outside for the bunny rabbits or in your compost pile. Alternatively, you can keep the skin on if you like.

2. Peel slices of the zucchini lengthwise with your potato peeler.

3. When you reach the seeds, then turn your zucchini and do the other side. Repeat on all sides, never going into the seed area. Toss the core to the bunnies or compost as well.

4. Place the noodles in a colander that sits over a bowl and sprinkle them with salt. Let them sit for about 20 minutes to sweat and drip off excess liquid.

5. Then wrap the noodles in a paper towel and squeeze gently to get remaining liquid out.

6. Melt the coconut oil in a skillet.

7. Add the noodles to the skillet and sauté until tender (about six or seven minutes). Stir frequently to prevent sticking and burning and don't overcook or they will get too soft.

Options

- A mandolin can be used instead of a potato peeler to get thicker slices that can be used to replace lasagna noodles. My lasagna recipe on page 108 uses cabbage as the noodle, but zucchini is another option.

- A cheese grater could be used instead of a potato peeler to make little noodles. Place the zucchini on the counter and take the grater across it lengthwise. Again, stopping when you hit the seed and turning to the other side.

Serve With

1. Just plain noodles in butter, salt, and pepper as a side to any meat dish.

2. Meatballs and spaghetti sauce.

3. Noodle casseroles and chicken noodle soup.

4. As a side topped with cherry tomatoes and chopped onion.

5. As a replacement for the noodle in any noodle or pasta dish.

6. Can be used in hot or cold noodle dishes.

Garlic Roasted Broccoli and/or Cauliflower

INGREDIENTS

1 lb of broccoli and/or cauliflower	2 tbsp coconut oil melted
1 tsp garlic powder	Salt and pepper to taste

Instructions

1. Preheat oven to 425.

2. Grease a baking sheet with a little bit of the oil.

3. Spread the broccoli and/or cauliflower the across baking sheet in a single layer.

4. Coat with remaining oil and toss to cover thoroughly.

5. Sprinkle with salt, pepper, and garlic powder and toss again.

6. Roast for about 15 to 20 minutes.

Spicy Guacamole

INGREDIENTS

3 medium avocados

½ cup chopped red onion

½ cup chopped cilantro

2 tbsp fresh lemon or lime juice

1 tbsp crushed red chili peppers

Salt and pepper to taste

Instructions

1. Cut the avocado in half at the equator.

2. Press the knife horizontally into the seed and pull it out.

3. Scoop out the insides and put it in a bowl.

4. Mash the avocado, but not too much. You want it to be a little chunky.

5. Stir in all the other ingredients.

6. Chill in the fridge.

Options

● Could add diced tomatoes if you like.

● Serve with veggies and meat dishes like burgers, meatloaf, chicken, steak, salads, or eggs.

Garlic Flavored Brussels Sprouts

INGREDIENTS

1 lb of Brussels Sprouts

2 or 3 tbsp of olive oil, butter, or ghee

1 tsp garlic powder

Salt and pepper to taste

Instructions

1. Steam the Brussels sprouts.

2. Pour them in a bowl.

3. Add oil, butter, or ghee, garlic powder, salt and pepper.

4. Serve warm.

5. During the holiday season, could add a $1/4$ cup of roasted chestnuts to the bowl.

Cabbage in Olive Oil

INGREDIENTS

1 serving of steamed cabbage	Salt and pepper to taste
1 tbsp of olive oil	

Instructions

1. Steam a head of cabbage.

2. Put the amount you want in a dish.

3. Sprinkle with olive oil.

4. Add salt and pepper to taste.

5. This dish is really good cold as well, which tastes great in the summer. After you steam your cabbage, stick it in the fridge overnight, then prepare the dish the same way the following day.

Options

- Can add a tablespoon of pumpkin seeds, sunflower seeds, or chia seeds.

- Other spices like onion, garlic powder, paprika, basil, oregano, red pepper, or dry mustard, could be added.

- Could use California blend (cauliflower, broccoli, and carrots) in place of cabbage.

- Walnut oil, sesame oil, macadamia oil, or high-oleic sunflower oil could be used instead of olive oil.

Cinnamon Cabbage

INGREDIENTS

1 head of shredded cabbage

2 tbsp coconut oil or butter or ghee

¼ to ½ tsp cinnamon

Salt and pepper to taste

Sprinkle of crushed red pepper

Instructions

1. Shred the head of cabbage with cheese grater.

2. Melt oil, butter, or ghee in skillet.

3. Add cabbage to the skillet and stir fry until soft.

4. Sprinkle with cinnamon, salt, pepper, and red pepper.

5. Serve with any meat dish. Tastes particularly great with sausage.

Options

- Could add chopped onion or bell peppers to the stir fry.
- Crushed red pepper could be omitted.

Lemon & Almond Green Bean Salad

INGREDIENTS

1 lb of cut green beans

2 tbsp of lemon juice

2 or 3 tbsp high-oleic sunflower oil

⅓ cup of sliced almonds

Salt and pepper to taste

Instructions

1. In a dry pan over medium-low heat toast sliced almonds. Stir frequently to avoid burning. After two minutes, almonds will smell fragrant. Set almonds aside.

2. Steam the green beans.

3. Place steamed beans in a bowl.

4. Mix lemon juice, salt, pepper, and oil together in a separate bowl.

5. Pour lemon and oil mixture over the green beans and toss to coat thoroughly.

6. Add almonds and toss.

7. Put in fridge and chill.

Options

● Could add chopped green onion.

● Roasted chestnuts could replace almonds at the holidays.

INGREDIENTS

1 10 oz bag of chopped kale	1 tsp garlic powder
2 tbsp olive oil	1 tsp onion powder
	Salt and pepper to taste

Instructions

1. Steam the kale until desired tenderness.

2. Place in a bowl.

3. Mix the oil, garlic powder, onion powder, salt, and pepper in a separate bowl, then pour it over the kale.

4. Toss kale to coat thoroughly.

Options

● Could add sliced cherry tomatoes, chopped tomatoes, or olives.

● Goes great with lamb, meat loaf, turkey loaf, or most any other meat dish.

● The kale could be eaten raw instead of steamed, if your gastrointestinal tract permits.

Refreshing Cucumber and Avocado Salad

INGREDIENTS

1 or 2 cucumbers

1 avocado

1 tbsp of lime juice

2 or 3 tbsp walnut oil or high-oleic sunflower oil

1 or 2 tbsp fresh parsley chopped

Salt and pepper to taste

Instructions

1. Slice the cucumbers and put them in a bowl.

2. Cut the avocado in half at the equator and remove the seed by pressing into it with the knife, twisting, and lifting.

3. Slice the avocado into thick slices and then dice the slices into little chunks.

4. Add avocado to bowl of cucumbers.

5. Combine oil, lime juice, parsley, pepper, and salt and pour over cucumbers and avocado.

6. Chill before serving.

Options

- Add chopped tomatoes or sliced cherry tomatoes.
- Chopped onion or green onion can be included.
- Could top with a little shredded cheese for a treat now and then.
- Sunflower or walnut oil can be replaced with other preferred oil (olive, macadamia, sesame, avocado).
- For a little variety, you can mash the avocado instead of cutting it into chucks.
- Delicious summer dish that goes great with burgers.

Basic Dressing

INGREDIENTS

¼ cup lemon juice

½ cup extra virgin olive oil

½ tsp dill

Salt and pepper to taste

Instructions

1. Mix all ingredients together in a container with a lid.

2. Shake vigorously and serve.

Options

- Add garlic powder or crushed garlic.

- Add dijon mustard.

- Add chopped parsley.

- Onion powder, chopped onions, or green onion could be included.

- Could use another oil in place of the olive oil, like high-oleic sunflower, avocado, walnut, or sesame.

- Lime could replace the lemon.

- A couple tablespoons of mashed avocado could thicken it up a bit and make it richer.

- Lemon juice could be replaced with apple cider vinegar, if this is not intolerable. If doing so, change ratio to one part apple cider vinegar to three parts oil.

- If you like a little sweetness in your dressing, you could add a dash of stevia.

Tangy Cucumbers

INGREDIENTS

1 or 2 cucumbers

Basic Dressing Recipe on page 121

2 tbsp fresh parsley chopped

Salt and pepper

Instructions

1. Dice cucumbers and place them in a bowl.

2. Dress with Basic Dressing until well coated.

3. Add parsley, salt, and pepper and mix thoroughly.

4. Put in the fridge and chill before serving.

Options

- Additional spices or herbs of your choice could be used, like minced garlic, chopped onion, or rosemary, cilantro, or thyme.

- Diced tomatoes or sliced cherry tomatoes could be added. Thinly sliced onion could be added as well.

- Great dish in the summer and goes well with about anything.

Green Beans in Herbs

INGREDIENTS

1 lb of french cut green beans

1 tsp basil

1 tsp oregano

½ tsp garlic powder

1 tsp onion flakes

Juice of ½ a lemon

2 or 3 tbsp of olive oil

Salt and pepper to taste

Instructions

1. Steam your green beans and put them in a bowl.

2. Add herbs, lemon, olive oil, salt, and pepper and toss.

3. Can be eaten warm or cold.

Options

- A different oil (walnut, sesame, macadamia, avocado, high-oleic sunflower) could replace olive oil.

- Can use butter instead of oil, if desired, for a different taste. If butter is used, will want to eat while warm.

- You can add any other herb you desire.

- Green beans are pretty versatile and go well with most meat dishes.

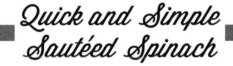

Quick and Simple Sautéed Spinach

INGREDIENTS

1 bag of chopped spinach	2 tbsp butter
2 tbsp finely chopped garlic	Salt and pepper to taste

Instructions

1. Melt the butter in a skillet.

2. Add as much spinach to the pan that will fit comfortably without being packed and the garlic and stir it around a bit to coat with butter.

3. Cover with a lid and cook for 3 to 5 minutes.

4. Take off the lid and stir.

5. Cover with the lid and cook for 3 to 5 more minutes, until spinach looks wilted.

6. Remove from the stove, put it on the plate and sprinkle with salt and pepper.

Options

- Could use ghee or coconut oil instead of butter.

- A touch of olive oil or lemon juice can be added after cooking.

- Additional spices or herbs of your choice could be included.

Chunky Celery Soup

INGREDIENTS

1 or 2 bunches of celery

1 or 2 carrots

½ cup of green onion

2 tbsp or so of oil of your choice
(olive, high-oleic sunflower,
avocado, walnut or sesame)

Salt and pepper to taste

2 tbsp chives

Instructions

1. Steam the celery, carrots, and green onion in steamer.

2. Then put in a blender or food processor with the oil, salt, and pepper.

3. Blend until desired consistency, I prefer to leave it a little chunky.

4. Pour in a bowl.

5. Garnish with chives.

6. Can be eaten warm or cold, but this one is better when warm.

Simple Zucchini Soup

INGREDIENTS

2 or 3 lbs of peeled zucchini

1 carrot

2 tbsp or so of oil of your choice
(I like walnut, as it gives it a slightly
sweet taste, but olive is good too)

½ cup of chopped leeks,
onion, or green onion

1 tbsp chives

Salt and pepper to taste

Instructions

1. Peel the skin off the zucchini.

2. Steam the zucchini, carrots, and leeks or onions in a steamer. Reserve steaming liquid.

3. Then put in a blender or food processor and add oil and salt.

4. Blend until smooth and creamy. Use reserved steaming liquid to thin out if soup is too thick.

5. Pour in a bowl.

6. Sprinkle with chives and pepper.

7. Can be eaten warm or cold. I like to have my first bowl warm and then eat the leftovers cold. It's a great cold soup on a hot summer's day.

8. Goes well with meatloaf and chicken.

Cream of Broccoli Soup

INGREDIENTS

2 or 3 lbs of broccoli

2 tbsp or so of oil of your choice
(olive, high-oleic sunflower,
avocado, walnut or sesame)

Salt and pepper to taste

Instructions

1. Steam the broccoli in a steamer. Reserve steamer liquid.

2. Then put it in a blender or food processor with oil, salt, and pepper. Add steamer liquid as needed for desired consistency.

3. Blend until creamy.

4. Pour in a bowl.

5. Can be eaten warm or cold. Again, I like this one warm for the first bowl and cold for the leftovers and cold is a great dish in the summer.

Options

- Could add leeks, onions, or carrots to the steamer.

Rich and Creamy Cauliflower Soup

INGREDIENTS

1 head of cauliflower

2 tbsp or so of oil of your choice
(I like walnut for this too, but each
one can give different flavor)

½ cup of leeks, onions,
or green onion

1 tbsp lemon juice

Salt and pepper to taste

2 tbsp of fresh parsley

Instructions

1. Steam the cauliflower and leeks or onions in a steamer. Reserve steamer liquid.

2. Then put in a blender with the oil, lemon juice, pepper and salt. Use reserved liquid to adjust desired consistency.

3. Blend until smooth and creamy.

4. Pour in a bowl.

5. Garnish with parsley.

6. Can be eaten warm or cold. I like to eat my first bowl warm and then the leftovers cold. This is also a great cold soup on a hot summer's day.

Options

- Could add rosemary, thyme, or cilantro for a more spicy flavor.

- Chives could be used as garnish instead of parsley.

- Leaks/onions could be omitted or replaced with a carrot.

- Lemon juice can be omitted if needed.

Mock Mashed Potatoes

INGREDIENTS

1 head of cauliflower

2 tbsp or so of one of the following
(butter, ghee, or oil of your choice)

Salt and pepper to taste

1 tbsp parsley

Instructions

1. Steam a head of cauliflower.

2. Put it in a bowl and add the oil or butter or ghee.

3. Add salt and pepper.

4. Mash with a hand potato masher to desired consistency (best if you like them a little chunky).

5. You can use a mixer once it is mashed a little bit by hand, if you want a smoother consistency.

6. Mix until it looks like mashed potatoes.

7. Alternatively, you could put it in the blender or food processor for a very smooth texture.

8. Top with a little parsley.

9. Use in place of mashed potatoes.

Options

- Could top with chives instead of parsley.

- Top with a teaspoon of butter or ghee.

I'm in Nirvana Sweet Potato

INGREDIENTS

1 sweet potato

½ tsp cinnamon

Sprinkle of nutmeg

Dash of salt

2 or 3 tbsp of butter at room temperature

1 tbsp of chopped pecans

Instructions

1. Preheat oven to 350.

2. Wash off a sweet potato.

3. Put it in a small dish with a lid or directly on the baking rack of the oven. Poke two or three times with a fork.

4. Bake it just like you would a white potato for about an hour or until soft.

5. Take it out, put it on a plate and slice it open lengthwise.

6. Mix cinnamon, nutmeg, and salt together with butter in a bowl.

7. Smother sweet potato with compound butter and then sprinkle with pecans.

8. Enjoy Nirvana.

9. This dish is so versatile it can be used as both a side dish or a dessert. Instead of candied yams that are pumped full of added sugar, I love to have it with my Thanksgiving dinner. Alternatively, it's so delicious that it can make a good replacement for pie.

10. There are many different types of sweet potatoes that vary in color and they are often confused for yams and vice versa. I prefer the ones that are a pale yellow outside and a little deeper yellow on the inside over the orange varieties, because I think they have superior taste and texture.

Options

- Instead of baking, you could boil, steam, or grill the sweet potato, which will provide a variety of different flavors and textures. I prefer baking, because it retains more flavor that way.

- Butter could be replaced with ghee, but I think it's more divine with butter.

- If you want to eliminate the dairy, or want to make this 100 percent paleo, then you could use coconut oil, walnut oil, or high-oleic sunflower oil, instead of the butter or ghee, but again it is most heavenly with the butter.

- Please note that sweet potatoes are a very high-carb food that will spike blood sugar and neurotransmitters, feed candida and SIBO, and fuel sugar and carb addiction, like any other carb. Therefore, they should be reserved for special occasions and treats, not eaten on a frequent basis. I include them in this cookbook primarily so you have an alternative to candied yams on the holidays, not as a green light for regular consumption. However, they are lower in carbs than the regular potato, so if potatoes are desired, the sweet potato is a better choice.

- On another note, sweet potatoes can be used in all the same ways as a white potato. They can be fried like hash browns, cut into french fries, mashed, etc.

Celery Sticks Snackers

CHOICE ONE

INGREDIENTS

2 celery stalks   2 tbsp of macadamia butter

Instructions

1. Wash celery sticks and put them on a plate.

2. Fill the stalk with macadamia butter.

CHOICE TWO

INGREDIENTS

2 celery stalks   Dash of cayenne, onion
1 avocado   powder, and garlic powder

Salt and pepper to taste

Instructions

1. Wash your celery sticks and put them on a plate.

2. Cut the avocado in half at the equator, remove the seed by pressing the knife into it, twisting, and lifting.

3. Scoop out the insides and put it in a bowl.

4. Mash the avocado to desired consistency with a fork.

5. Add spices, salt, and pepper and mix with fork.

6. Fill the stalk with the avocado mixture.

Options

- Macadamia butter could be replaced with any nut or seed butter you desire. For example, sunflower butter and almond butter are also very good.

- You could add any other spices you desire to the mashed avocado for a variety of different flavors.

- If you permit dairy, then cream cheese mixed with your choice of spices could be used in place of the macadamia butter or avocado as well.

- Can be used as a side dish, snack, or dessert.

Oven Roasted Asparagus

INGREDIENTS

1 lb of asparagus spears (trimmed and washed)

2 tbsp butter, ghee, or coconut oil melted

Salt and coarse ground pepper to taste

1 tsp garlic powder

Instructions

1. Preheat oven to 425.

2. Line a baking dish with parchment paper.

3. Place the asparagus in the dish in a single layer.

4. Drizzle the butter over top of it.

5. Sprinkle with salt, pepper, and garlic powder.

6. Toss them around to coat them thoroughly.

7. Bake for about 6 or 8 minutes and then turn with fork and bake another 6 to 8 minutes.

Options

- Could sprinkle with lemon juice after they are roasted.

- Other herbs and spices could be sprinkled on after cooking as well, like thyme or parsley.

- Onion powder or other preferred spices could be added to the salt and pepper prior to cooking.

- Grated cheese on top right before serving is another possibility.

Cynthia's Barbecue Sauce

INGREDIENTS

6 oz of tomato paste

2 tbsp butter or ghee melted

½ tsp garlic powder

¼ tsp pepper

3 or 4 tbsp of apple cider vinegar
(see resource section)

½ tsp dry mustard

¼ to ½ tsp cinnamon

½ tsp onion powder

2 tsp of red chili pepper

1 cup of water

Stevia to desired sweetness

Instructions

1. Whisk all ingredients together in a saucepot over medium-low heat. Simmer for 30 minutes to an hour to integrate flavors.

2. Brush it onto whatever meat dish you are preparing (e.g. chicken, ribs, shredded beef).

3. Alternatively, can be used as a dip for things like chicken tenders.

Sweet or Spicy Butter Balls

INGREDIENTS FOR SWEET

1 stick butter

1 tsp vanilla

Dash of stevia

Dash of salt

Instructions for Sweet

1. Blend all the ingredients together in a blender or food processor.

2. Scoop by heaping tsps or a small ice cream scoop onto parchment paper and roll each one into a ball.

3. Chill in the refrigerator.

Options for Sweet

- Could roll each of the balls in almond meal.

INGREDIENTS FOR SPICY

1 stick butter	1 tsp garlic oil
1 tbsp of chives, basil, and oregano mixed together	Dash of salt

Instructions for Spicy

1. Blend all the ingredients together in a blender or food processor.

2. Scoop by heaping teaspoons or a small ice cream scoop onto parchment paper and roll each one into a ball.

3. Chill in the refrigerator.

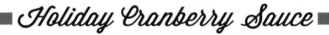

Holiday Cranberry Sauce

INGREDIENTS

8 oz of cranberries	Stevia to taste
½ cup unsweetened cherry juice or apple juice	

Instructions

1. Wash cranberries and pick out the bad ones.

2. Put them in a small sauce pan with the juice and stevia.

3. Simmer over medium heat and stir occasionally until berries burst open and turn saucy (about 15 minutes).

Options

- Could add a little cinnamon.

- Water could be used in place of the fruit juice to lower the sugar content and then increase the stevia to sweeten.

Roasted Zucchini & Yellow Squash

INGREDIENTS

2 tbsp coconut oil melted

2 green zucchini

2 yellow squash

Salt and pepper to taste

1 tsp parsley

Instructions

1. Preheat oven to 425 degrees.

2. Grease a baking sheet with 1 teaspoon of oil and place in the oven.

3. Cut zucchini and squash into 1-inch slices and put them in a big bowl.

4. Sprinkle with remaining oil and toss to coat.

5. Sprinkle with salt and pepper.

6. Being careful with the hot baking sheet, spead the vegetables evenly and place back inside the oven. Having the baking sheet preheated will sear the vegetables initially rather than steam and give you more golden brown vegetables.

7. Roast for 10 minutes, then toss, and roast for another 10 minutes.

8. Take out of the oven and sprinkle with parsley.

Options

- Could sprinkle with lemon juice, onion or garlic powder, basil, thyme, or other spice prior to roasting.

- Mixed bell peppers could be included as well.

- These can be used instead of noodles and they taste great topped with tomato sauce.

- During the holiday season, you could add a $1/2$ cup of roasted chestnuts before serving.

DESSERTS

Dairy-Free Whipped Cream

INGREDIENTS

1 can of full-fat coconut milk

Several dashes of stevia

1 tsp of vanilla

Instructions

1. Put a can of coconut milk in the fridge at least overnight, but longer is better. I give it several days.

2. Chill a stainless steel bowl in the freezer for a half hour.

3. Take can of coconut milk out of fridge. Do not shake the can, because you do not want to mix the fat back in with the liquid. You will see that the fat has risen to the top when you open it.

4. Scoop the fat out and leave the liquid in the can.

5. Mix with mixer for about 2 minutes or so. Until it looks like whipped cream.

6. Stir in vanilla and stevia with a fork or mix again for another 30 seconds or so.

7. Serve on favorite fruit or any other dish that calls for whipped cream.

8. Caution: this is very filling and it slides down your throat so easy that it is easy to overeat before you realize it and then you feel too full. Quit eating a little before you start to feel full. I have overdone it on several occasions and paid a painful price.

9. Please note that this is a very low-carb food (only 1 gram per tablespoon), and therefore, it can be eaten by itself if fruit produces too many symptoms for you. Additionally, it can be eaten more freely than other dessert recipes and will satiate many carb cravings.

Alternative Method

- Instead of using coconut milk, you can buy coconut cream. Coconut cream is in a smaller can, they have already removed the milk portion for you, and it contains nothing but the cream. Then follow the directions for whipping the same. Don't confuse coconut cream with coconut butter. See resource section for brand of coconut cream.

Options

- Replace the vanilla with a different flavor like orange, lemon, cherry, etc.

Pears and Raspberries

Raspberries and pears taste particularly delicious when combined together and can be served in a variety of different ways.

INGREDIENTS

1 pear   ½ cup of raspberries

Instructions

- Option 1—Slice a pear in a bowl and mix with a ¹/₂ cup of fresh raspberries and eat.

- Option 2—Puree the pear and raspberries in a blender or food processor into an applesauce consistency and warm it up a bit in a saucepan or chill it and eat cold.

- Option 3—Puree the pears and raspberries together and then freeze it into a sorbet.

- Option 4—Bake them together in a covered dish in the oven for 30 minutes at 350 degrees.

The Real Deal Whipped Cream

INGREDIENTS

1 8 oz carton of full-fat heavy whipping cream (I prefer Organic Valley brand)

1 tsp of vanilla

Several dashes of stevia

Instructions

1. Chill a stainless steel bowl in the freezer for a half hour.

2. Pour cream in the bowl.

3. Mix with mixer for about 2 or 3 minutes. Until it begins to form soft peaks.

4. Fold in vanilla and stevia with a fork and mix again for another minute or so, until it forms firm peaks.

5. Be careful not to mix too long. The texture begins to turn into something like cream cheese in just a minute or so after it reaches the whipped cream stage.

6. Serve on favorite fruit or any other dish that calls for whipped cream.

7. Real cream contains almost no carbs as well (about .04 per table-spoon), so this food can be eaten by itself, or sprinkled with a few nuts, if fruit produces too many symptoms for you. Additionally, it can be eaten more freely than other dessert recipes and will also satiate many carb cravings.

8. This is also very easy to accidentally overeat and feel too full, so be careful to quit eating before you begin to feel full.

Options

- You can add a variety of different flavors to the whipped cream instead of, or in addition to, the vanilla, so feel free to be creative and experiment. For example, a little pumpkin pie spice is good around the holidays and can be served on apple or pear slices. Cherry, orange, maple, or almond flavoring would be tasty as well.

- If you add any other substance once it has already formed firm peaks, then you must fold it in gently so it won't lose its whipped cream texture.

Cinnamon Baked Pears with Pecans

INGREDIENTS

1 pear	¼ cup chopped pecans
¼ tsp vanilla	Dash of cinnamon

Instructions

1. Put pear in a baking dish with a little water and cut a slit down through its middle.

2. Sprinkle with vanilla, pecans, and cinnamon.

3. Cover with a lid and bake at 350 until soft (about 30 minutes).

4. Eat warm.

Options

- Alternatively, this recipe can be done with an apple and walnuts instead and is just as good.

- Could add a handful of cranberries before baking.

- Can top with the real deal whipped cream on page 137 or dairy-free whipped cream on page 135 if you desire, but it's delicious without.

- Pecans could be replaced with chestnuts, but this will increase carb content somewhat.

- Pumpkin seeds or sunflower seeds could be used instead of nuts.

- Nuts or seeds could be added after the baking, instead of baking with, to avoid oxidation of nuts or seeds.

Banana Bites

METHOD ONE:
BANANA CREAM BITES

INGREDIENTS

1 small ripe banana

½ cup whipped cream from page 135 or page 137

2 tbsp chopped nuts (pecans, almonds, macadamia, walnuts)

Instructions

1. Slice the bananas in pieces about a half inch in width and put on a plate.

2. Put a dollop of whipped cream on top of each banana slice.

3. Sprinkle each one with a few chopped nuts.

4. Eat as is or chill for a bit and serve.

Options

- Sprinkle with nutmeg or cinnamon.

- Could melt unsweetened carob over the top of it for a special treat on occasion (please see note on carob on page 54 and resource section).

- Put them in the freezer for 10 minutes for a cool treat in the summer.

- Omit the nuts.

- Chia seeds, sunflower seeds, or pumpkin seeds could be used instead of chopped nuts.

- Could put nutty crust from page 149 into mini muffin liners and place place bananas and cream inside them instead.

METHOD TWO:
NUTTY BANANA COCONUT BITES

INGREDIENTS

1 small ripe banana   ¼ cup of nut meal

¼ cup of coconut butter

Instructions

1. Slice banana into pieces about a half inch in width and put them on a plate.

2. Put coconut butter in a small bowl.

3. Dip the banana slices into coconut butter.

4. Then dip the banana slices into nut meal.

5. Serve.

Options

- Sprinkle with cinnamon or nutmeg.

METHOD THREE:
SUNFLOWER DIPPED BANANA BITES

INGREDIENTS

1 small ripe banana   2 tbsp sunflower butter

Instructions

1. Peel banana.

2. Put sunflower butter in bowl.

3. Dip the banana into the sunflower butter and bite. Dip and bite. Dip and bite.

Options

- Could add cinnamon, vanilla, or nutmeg to the sunflower butter before dipping.

Spiced Peaches and Cream Paradise

INGREDIENTS

1 bowl of sliced peaches (chilled)

2 tbsp whipped cream
from page 137

1 tbsp of chopped walnuts

Couple dashes of cinnamon
and nutmeg

Instructions

1. Add a dash or two of cinnamon to the whipped cream and fold it in gently. Alternatively, you can add the cinnamon at the same time you add the vanilla when you make the whipped cream.

2. Sprinkle a couple dashes of cinnamon and nutmeg on the chilled peaches and stir them around to coat them completely.

3. Place the whipped cream on top of the peaches.

4. Sprinkle it with chopped walnuts and serve.

Options

- You can use the dairy-free whipped cream on page 135 in place of the whipped cream if you desire, but I think it tastes best with the real deal whipped cream.

- I have tried both pecans and walnuts and either one taste delicious. You could try almonds or macadamias as well for variety.

- This is so completely satisfying and scrumptious that you will truly feel like you are in paradise and it will also derail an intense carb craving.

- Sunflower or chia seeds could be used instead of nuts.

Baked Apple Slices with Chestnuts

INGREDIENTS

2 apples

¼ cup chopped chestnuts

2 tbsp of water

½ tsp cinnamon

1 tbsp butter, ghee, or coconut oil

Dash of salt

Whipped cream from page 135 or 137

Instructions

1. Preheat oven to 400.

2. Cut apples into slices.

3. Grease a baking dish with butter, ghee, or coconut oil.

4. Add apples and chestnuts to pan and sprinkle with water, cinnamon, and salt.

5. Bake for about 30 or 40 minutes, until tender.

6. Top with whipped cream from page 135 or 137.

Options

- Sprinkle with vanilla and/or nutmeg in addition to or instead of cinnamon.

- Water could be replaced with lemon juice.

Vanilla Almond Butter

INGREDIENTS

2 tbsp of almond butter

½ tsp of vanilla with a glycerin base, not alcohol (glycerin is sweet by nature so it adds a little sweetness)

Dash of salt

Instructions

1. Combine almond butter, vanilla, and salt in a bowl.

2. Stir.

3. Eat by itself or serve with your favorite fruit.

4. I particularly love this served with raspberries, but peaches are good too.

5. Has about 6 grams of carbs per serving, so it is acceptable for those staying under 50 grams per day.

Options

- You could use any type of nut butter you prefer in place of the almond butter. Pecan is also very good and tastes almost like candy.

- Sunflower butter or pumpkin seed butter could replace nut butter and the sunflower butter option also tastes almost like candy.

Mixed Berries and Nuts

INGREDIENTS

5 or 6 fresh or thawed frozen strawberries, blueberries, blackberries

¼ teaspoon vanilla

¼ cup chopped walnuts

Instructions

1. Slice the berries and put them in a bowl.

2. Drizzle with vanilla and stir.

3. Sprinkle with crushed walnuts.

Options

- Walnuts could be replaced with any nut you desire.

- Dish could be topped with whipped cream from page 135 or 137.

- Could be added to a cup of full-fat yogurt on occasion.

Sunflower Macaroons

INGREDIENTS

1 cup full-fat shredded coconut

½ cup sunflower butter

½ tsp vanilla

Dash of stevia

Instructions

1. Pre-heat oven to 325 degrees.

2. Spread out half of the coconut on sheet tray, place in oven to toast. Check after 5 minutes, mix around. When tips of coconut are lightly browned and coconut is fragrant, pull from oven. Watch carefully, as it burns quickly.

3. Take the other half of coconut and place in a food processor with sunflower butter, vanilla, and stevia. Process until smooth.

4. Transfer to a bowl and fold in toasted coconut.

5. Separate into four equal size cookies and place on parchment paper. Press into desired shape with spoon and fingers.

6. Stick in the freezer for a few hours until firm.

7. Keep leftovers in the fridge or freezer and they are just as good for a couple days.

8. Each cookie has about 10 grams of carbs, so if you eat only one, this is a dessert that you can indulge in even if you are staying under 50 grams per day.

Options

- These cookies have a slight crunch. If you would like them to have a softer and smoother texture, then you could skip the roasting step and use only unroasted coconut. Then process in the food processor until the batter is smooth.

Cherries Drizzled in Almond Butter

INGREDIENTS

Bowl of cherries (I like to buy frozen
ones and then let them thaw,
because they have a softer texture)

1 or 2 tbsp of almond butter

Instructions

1. Put cherries in a bowl and drizzle with almond butter.

Options

- These two flavors together (almonds and cherry) really compliment one another and are exquisite. However, you could use macadamia butter or walnut butter instead of almond.

- Could pour melted carob over top (please see note on carob on page 54 and resource section).

Strawberries & Cream

INGREDIENTS

1 bowl of strawberries

2 tbsp whipped cream
from page 135 or 137

1 tbsp crushed walnuts

½ tsp of vanilla

Instructions

1. If you use fresh strawberries, stick them in the freezer for about an hour to chill them. If you use frozen strawberries, then let them thaw until soft, but still cold.

2. Put the strawberries in a bowl.

3. Sprinkle them with nuts.

4. Top with the real deal whipped cream from page 137 or the dairy-free whipped cream from page 135. Either one tastes great.

Options

- Of course this recipe could be done with blueberries, or any other fruit you like. I tried blueberries, but I liked strawberries much better.

- This dish is a very satiating dessert. If you are having a craving for a carb it will really hit the spot. You will not walk away from the dinner table feeling the least bit hungry.

Dipped Dates

INGREDIENTS

1 or 2 tbsp of macadamia
butter

3 or 4 dates

Instructions

1. Put your macadamia butter in a bowl, dip your dates into it, and eat.

Options

- Macadamia butter can be replaced with almond butter or any other preferred nut butter.
- You can use figs in place of the dates for a change.
- Sunflower butter could be used instead of nut butter.
- Could roll in shredded coconut after dipping in nut butter.
- Coconut butter could be used instead of nut or seed butter.

Caution

This is another treat that is very good for satisfying intense cravings for carbohydrates. It's hard to overeat or binge on a whole fruit treat like this, because it is so satisfying and you get full fast. However, do remember that dates are exceptionally high in sugar and should be reserved for rare occasions or to satiate an overwhelming craving.

Peach Crumble

INGREDIENTS

1 bags of sliced peaches
(I use Woodstock Organics
frozen peaches and thaw
them out. See resource
section for other options.)

1 tsp cinnamon

¼ tsp of vanilla

1 cup organic almond meal
(I use Blue Mountain Organics Raw
Almond Meal, which is incredibly
rich in flavor and fresh. Be sure
you don't use almond "flour.")

2 tbsp of melted butter

Dash of stevia

Whipped cream from page 135 or 137

Instructions

1. Preheat oven to 375.

2. Place the peaches in the baking dish and sprinkle with vanilla, half the cinnamon, and a dash of stevia.

3. Mix the butter and almond meal together with a fork or pastry knife until you have a nice crumbly texture.

4. Stir in the other half of cinnamon and a dash of stevia.

5. Sprinkle the topping on top of the peaches.

6. Bake for 30 minutes.

7. Let cool before eating.

8. Top with whipped cream from page 135 or page 137.

9. I ate some while it was still very warm, and although it was divine in flavor, it didn't hold its shape too well. So be sure to let it cool before eating. However, I put it in the fridge and ate the leftovers the next day and it held its shape very well and it was even more superb the second time around. So, you may find you want to make this dish the day before you plan to eat it.

10. Peach crumble could be a delicious addition to your menu at Thanksgiving, Christmas, or Easter, or at picnics and barbecues, or a special treat any time of year.

Options

- Apples, pears, or blueberries could be used instead of peaches. If blueberries are used, omit the cinnamon.

- Butter could be replaced with ghee or coconut oil.

INGREDIENTS

2 tbsp of softened room temperature butter

1 cup of nut meal (walnut, macadamia, almond, etc.)

Dash of salt and stevia

Instructions

1. Put all the ingredients into a bowl.

2. Cut the butter into the nut meal until it begins to form together and hold.

3. Use as you would a crust for anything. (pie, cheesecakes, etc.) It can be formed into a crust in a pie pan or muffin liners by pressing it down with your fingers or a spoon, or it can be crumbled across the top of something.

4. Can be eaten raw or baked, but remember baking oxidizes the nuts.

Options

- Butter can be replaced with coconut oil.

All-Purpose No-Bake Thumbprint Cookies

INGREDIENTS

¾ cup raw almond meal, coarsely ground, not fine like flour (I like Blue Mountain Organics Raw Almond Meal)

¼ cup almond butter

1 tsp vanilla

¼ cup coconut oil melted

1 cup full-fat shredded coconut

2 tbsp water with a dash of stevia

¼ cup unsweetened carob chips (add water as needed)

Instructions

1. Mix the coconut, almond meal, and almond butter together.

2. Add vanilla, coconut oil, and water. You may need to add a little more water to get the dough to stick together well.

3. Stick in a food processor until it sticks together, just a minute or two. You can mix with a fork instead, but processor works better.

4. Place rounded tbsp of mixture out onto a plate with parchment paper (about 7).

5. Wet your thumb or the back of a spoon and press into the center of each cookie, making a little concave.

6. Melt carob chips in a pan with a little water; add water as needed until it makes a texture that is like frosting.

7. Scoop carob out with a spoon and place inside the thumbprint of each cookie, filling the concave.

8. Cover and stick in the fridge for several hours.

9. Keep leftovers in the fridge. They are just as delicious the next day and will keep a couple days.

10. This is a really quick and easy recipe that produces a treat that is low-carb, very rich in flavor, has a great texture, and tastes delicious.

Alternative Method

1. Technically, the recipe above is not true paleo, because of the carob filling. However, as mentioned previously, a little carob on a special occasion will not be too detrimental and carob is always a better choice than chocolate, which is not true paleo either. Please read my note about carob on page 54 and chocolate on page 41.

2. If you wanted to make this recipe 100 percent paleo, you could use some kind of all fruit jelly for the filling instead of carob. Alternatively, a pecan, date paste, or fig paste could be used instead of the carob to fill the center as well.

3. To make date or fig paste, simply take one cup of dried dates or figs and cover with a half a cup of hot water and let sit for a minute or two. Then stick them in a food processor for a minute and you have a paste. Please note, that since dates and figs contain a significant amount of sugar, they will increase the carb content more than carob.

Options

- Carob powder can be used instead of carob chips. Mix powder and water together in a small saucepan and cook for a few minutes to make the desired consistency.

- Instead of pressing in the center and filling it with something, you could just omit this step and leave the cookies as they are when you first put them on the plate. They will be lower in carb this way.

- Other types of nut meal and nut butter could replace the almond meal and almond butter for a variety of different flavors.

- Sunflower butter could replace the nut butter.

- I make these cookies at Christmas, but you could use them for any occasion, like Valentine's Day or Easter, or just when the urge for a cookie strikes you. They also work great in the kid's lunchbox, for dessert, picnics, or road trips.

Pumpkin Pie Mousse

INGREDIENTS

4 tsp pumpkin puree (I like Farmer's Market brand, and it has a BPA free liner)

2 tbsp pecan butter (I love Blue Mountain Organics nut butter, they soak them for you)

Dash of stevia

Dash of pumpkin pie spice blend (cinnamon, ginger, nutmeg)

3 tbsp real deal whipped cream from page 137

Instructions

1. Mix the pumpkin, pecan butter, stevia, and spices together in a bowl.

2. Make the whipped cream as described on page 137.

3. Fold the whipped cream into the pumpkin mixture gently, until it is all mixed together and smooth and creamy. It only takes a minute or so.

4. Put in the fridge or freezer for just a bit to chill.

Options

- If you don't do dairy, then you can use the coconut based whipped cream from page 135, but I think it is more delightful with the real dairy whipped cream.

- Cinnamon could be used alone if you don't have any pumpkin pie spice blend on hand.

- Pecan butter could be replaced with walnut or almond butter for a little variety, but in my opinion, the combination of pecan and pumpkin is exquisite.

- This recipe is very low in carbs, (less than 10 grams per serving) so it is a nutritious dessert that can be enjoyed without guilt, exacerbation of symptoms, or fear of harming your health. It is so rich, creamy, and satiating that it will also work well to satisfy a carb craving. Not only that, it only takes about 10 minutes from start to finish to make, so it's quick and easy as well.

- This makes a great dish on Thanksgiving and the holiday season, and could actually replace the pumpkin pie, if you're looking for an alternative. However, it can be enjoyed any time of the year you might be in the mood for pumpkin. Leave it in the freezer for a while in the summer for a cooling off dish.

Basic Fruit Salad

INGREDIENTS

1 bag of frozen blackberries

1 bag of frozen blueberries

1 bag of frozen strawberries

1 bag of frozen cherries

1 fresh banana sliced

Instructions

1. Mix all these together in a bowl and let them sit covered in the fridge for several hours, preferably overnight, so they thaw and their juices can combine.

Options

- You can use any type of fruit you desire in place of what I've suggested, but the combination I suggested tastes particularly delicious together.

- Great for those summer picnics.

Strawberry and Banana Split Parfait

INGREDIENTS

1 small ripe banana

3 or 4 strawberries

Whipped Cream from
page 135 or 137

½ cup of chopped walnuts

1 cherry

Instructions

1. Slice the bananas and strawberries.

2. Place a dollop of whipped cream in the bottom of a parfait dish.

3. Place a layer of sliced strawberries and bananas.

4. Then a layer of chopped nuts.

5. Add another dollop of whipped cream on top of the nuts.

6. Then another layer of strawberries and bananas.

7. And another layer of chopped nuts.

8. Continue layering until you have one layer above the rim of the dish.

9. Last layer should be nuts.

10. Top with a whole cherry.

11. This is another very satiating dish that will work great if you have an overwhelming sugar or carb craving.

Options

- Could throw some blueberries in there if you like, which would look very festive on the Fourth of July.

Paleo Approved Candies

These healthy and scrumptious candy-like treats can be used on any holiday like Easter, Christmas, Valentine's Day, Halloween, birthday parties or any other occasion. They are not only melt in your mouth delicious, but they are quick and easy as well, and very low-carb.

However, do be aware that coconut butter and nuts can be a trigger food for binging in some people with sugar and carb addiction. I frequently work with people who are trying to overcome sugar and carb addiction, who switch their addictions to coconut, nuts, and seeds when they transition to a paleo diet. Sometimes it is just a temporary phase that passes once they have been eating paleo long enough to restore balance to their brain chemistry and endocrine system, but it can sabotage your diet if you're not aware and let it run rampant.

Lemon Drops

INGREDIENTS

¼ cup coconut butter
(soft at room temperature)

½ tsp lemon extract (can adjust
this for desired intensity of flavor)

Dash of salt

Unbleached mini muffin liners
(see resource section)

Instructions

1. Mix all ingredients together in a bowl.

2. Stick the bowl in the freezer for about 3 to 5 minutes, until it starts to get firm. (Keep an eye on it, because it doesn't take long before it gets too hard to work with.)

3. Take it out of the freezer and drop one teaspoon full of mixture into each mini muffin liner. If you want bigger drops, then use a tablespoon.

4. Stick in the freezer for about 15 or 20 minutes.

5. That's it. Take them out and eat them.

6. Store leftovers in the fridge or the freezer.

Options

- Orange extract could replace the lemon extract.

Cinnamon Drops

INGREDIENTS

¼ cup coconut butter
(soft at room temperature)

½ tsp cinnamon (can adjust this
for desired intensity of flavor)

Dash of salt

Instructions

1. Follow the instructions above for Lemon Drops.

Vanilla Drops

INGREDIENTS

¼ cup coconut butter
(soft at room temperature)

1 tsp vanilla

Dash of salt

Instructions

1. Repeat the instructions provided for Lemon Drops.

Macadamia Cremes

INGREDIENTS

4 tbsp of coconut butter
(soft at room temperature)

6 tbsp of macadamia butter

1 tsp vanilla

Dash of salt

Unbleached muffin liners
regular size

Instructions

1. Mix all the ingredients together in a bowl until creamy.

2. Distribute the mixture into five muffin liners, dividing it evenly between them.

3. Stick them in the freezer for about 3 hours.

4. Enjoy and keep any leftovers in the freezer.

5. These come out of the liner looking like Reese's Peanut Butter Cups. If you want mini Reese's size cups instead, then you could use mini muffin liners.

Almond Cremes

INGREDIENTS

½ cup coconut butter
(soft at room temperature)

⅔ cup almond butter

½ tsp almond extract

Dash of salt

Instructions

1. Repeat the instructions that are provided for Macadamia Cremes.

Maple Leaves

INGREDIENTS

¼ cup coconut butter
(soft at room temperature)

1 tsp maple flavor

Dash of salt

Instructions

1. Mix all the ingredients together in a bowl and pour into maple leaves candy molds.

2. Stick in the freezer until solid.

3. Store leftovers in fridge or freezer.

Options

● Could use any candy mold shape you desire.

Options for All the Coconut Candy Recipes

- Any of the coconut candy recipes can be poured into a candy mold or cookie cutter of any kind. Depending on which holiday you are celebrating, you could alter the shapes. So, you could essentially have them shaped as eggs, bunny rabbits, or chicks for Easter; and Xmas trees, snowmen, and bells for Christmas; a heart for Valentine's Day; and a witch or ghost for Halloween.

- You can replace the macadamia or almond butter with any other type of nut butter you prefer for many different versions.

- Different spices or flavors can be used as desired. For example, cinnamon or lemon could be replaced with orange, peppermint, cherry, etc.

- You can also decorate them, if you like, with chopped raisins, dried fruit, shredded coconut, or crushed nuts, prior to freezing.

- So feel free to be creative and come up with your own variations that will be a hit for you and/or your family.

- The cinnamon drops, lemon drops, vanilla drops, and maple leaves only contain about 3 grams of carbs per piece, or less, depending on how big you make the drops. The macadamia cremes contain about 5.6 grams of carbs per piece and the almond cremes only contain about 7 grams per piece.

- If you're really short on time, or you hate to bake, simply store a jar of coconut butter in the fridge where it will harden. Anytime the mood strikes you, just take a knife and cut out a small piece to savor. Be sure to stir it good before sticking in the fridge.

Mini Blueberry Cheesecakes

INGREDIENTS

6 oz of cream cheese

¾ cup blueberries
(room temperature)

¼ cup of butter

1 tsp vanilla extract

¼ tsp of stevia

Nutty crust from page 149

Regular size unbleached
muffin liners
(see resource section)

Instructions

1. Chop up blueberries in food processor for a few seconds and drain off the juice.

2. Put butter and cream cheese in a bowl and let sit for about an hour, until soft.

3. While you're waiting, cover the bottom of each muffin liner with a layer of the nutty crust mixture from page 149. Press it with your thumb or spoon to form a solid base that resembles a mini pie crust inside the muffin liner.

4. Mix blueberries, vanilla, and stevia together.

5. Mix cream cheese, butter, and stevia together with a fork or mixer until mixed thoroughly.

6. Add fruit mixture to cream cheese mixture and stir together with fork.

7. Drop a heaping tbsp of cream cheese mixture on top of nut lined muffin liners.

8. Put in the freezer for about 90 minutes.

9. Serve and delight.

10. Leftovers can be kept in freezer or fridge.

Options

- Could use strawberries, blackberries, raspberries, peaches, cherries, or pineapples instead of blueberries if you like.

- $1/2$ cup pumpkin puree and a $1/4$ to $1/2$ teaspoon of pumpkin pie spice could be used instead of blueberries for a holiday pumpkin cheesecake.

Raspberry Cobbler

INGREDIENTS

½ cup raspberries

3 tbsp almond meal

¼ tsp vanilla extract in glycerin base

Instructions

1. Put raspberries in bowl.

2. In a separate bowl, mix the almond meal and vanilla together thoroughly with a fork until it is a moist and crumbly mixture and looks something like granola.

3. Sprinkle the almond mixture over top of the raspberries and serve.

4. I like to use vanilla in a glycerin base, because the glycerin adds a little extra touch of sweetness that has no impact on candida, blood sugar, insulin, etc.

Options

- Blueberries and walnut meal could be used instead of raspberries and almond meal.

Nuts and Cream

INGREDIENTS

2 tbsp nut butter or chopped nuts, lightly salted (any nut or nut butter you prefer)

4 tbsp whipped cream

Instructions

1. Fold the nuts or nut butter into the cream.

2. Chill and serve.

Options

- Cinnamon, vanilla, cherry, almond, lemon, or peppermint flavoring could be added to the whipped cream or nuts.

- Sunflower butter or pumpkin seed butter could replace nut butter.

- Only has around 5 to 8 grams of carbs per serving, depending on what nuts you've used.

Simply Sautéed Fruit

INGREDIENTS

2 apples, pears, or peaches	2 or 3 tbsp butter, ghee, or coconut oil

Instructions

1. Slice preferred fruit into slices.

2. Melt butter or oil in skillet.

3. Add fruit slices.

4. Cook and stir frequently until tender (several minutes or longer if want very soft).

Options

- Could have one individual fruit, or combine all three for an autumn blend.

- Top with chopped nuts or seeds and/or whipped cream from page 137 or 135 after finished cooking.

- Sprinkle with cinnamon, vanilla, or nutmeg.

- A few raisins could be included.

- You could use any other fruit you like, but apples, pears and peaches sauté beautifully.

Chestnut Puree

INGREDIENTS

5 oz roasted chestnuts (I buy them already roasted in a foil bag. See resource section.)

1 cup full-fat coconut milk

¼ tsp vanilla

Dash of salt

Stevia to taste

INGREDIENTS

1. Put chestnuts in a small saucepan and cover with coconut milk.

2. Bring to a boil and then reduce to medium-low and simmer for about 20 to 25 mins until soft and most of the milk has evaporated.

3. Pour the mixture through a sieve or fine mesh to separate from remaining liquid, but save the liquids.

4. Put the nuts into a food processor with the vanilla, salt, and stevia and blend until smooth.

5. Add some of the liquid back, a little bit at a time, and process again until you get your desired consistency.

6. Store it in the refrigerator and it can be used as a replacement for other seeds or nuts in other recipes like ice cream or soup.

Options

- Coconut milk can be replaced with heavy cream, if you permit dairy.

- Water can be used instead of coconut milk.

- Stevia, vanilla, and salt can be omitted for a less sweet and plain flavor.

- Do remember that chestnuts are higher in carbs than most nuts, so it should be eaten in moderation.

Gesztenyepüre
(Hungarian Chestnut Puree)

INGREDIENTS

Chestnut puree from page 162   1 cherry

Whipped cream from page 135 or 137

Instructions

1. Cover the bottom of a dessert dish with a dollop or two of whipped cream.

2. Place a couple tbsp of chestnut puree on top of the whipped cream.

3. Add another dollop or two of whipped cream on top of puree.

4. Top with a cherry.

Options

- Could put melted carob over top of chestnut puree before the last layer of whipped cream as a special treat (please see note on carob on page 54 and resource section).

Coconut Pops

INGREDIENTS

1 can full-fat coconut milk   Dash of stevia

1 tbsp vanilla

Instructions

1. Shake the can of coconut milk.

2. Open it and stir in the vanilla and stevia.

3. Pour it into freezer pop molds and stick them in the freezer until frozen.

4. Only about 7 grams of carbs per pop depending on size of mold.

Options

- Could add chopped nuts and/or pieces of fruit (strawberries, blueberries, bananas, cherries etc.) before freezing.

- Vanilla extract can be replaced with any flavor you desire, like peppermint, vanilla, maple, cherry, or almond.

- Chia seeds could be included.

- Add carob powder to make a fudgesicle.

Vanilla Bean Banana "Ice Cream"

INGREDIENTS

1 ripe banana

1 vanilla bean

1 or 2 tbsp of macadamia nut butter (could use almond, cashew, pecan, etc.)

Instructions

1. Put a banana in the blender or mash and stir with a fork in a bowl.

2. Add one or two tbsp of your preferred nut butter. I really love this recipe with macadamia butter; it is so smooth, rich, and creamy. But almond, cashew, or pecan are good as well. You can have a different one each time for a little variety.

3. Slice a vanilla bean in half with a sharp knife lengthwise, then scrape the middle of it with the back of your knife to remove the seeds and sprinkle into your bowl.

4. Blend together gently with a fork until smooth and creamy.

5. Put in the freezer for several hours or until it reaches desired consistency.

Alternative Method

- This method uses the exact same ingredients as above, but uses a different set of instructions for preparation, which results in a slightly different texture and flavor. You may find you like one better than the other, or enjoy alternating between the options for a little variety. Sometimes it's a matter of which one is more convenient at the time. If you happen to have a frozen banana already on hand, it's easy to take it out of the freezer and throw in the blender without any planning ahead. On the other hand, if the desire for ice cream strikes you, but you only have fresh bananas on hand, then the second method will come in handy. Either way, the desire can be fulfilled.

INGREDIENTS

1 frozen banana

1 or 2 tbsp of macadamia nut butter (could use almond, cashew, pecan etc.)

1 vanilla bean

Instructions

1. Peel and freeze your banana for 24 hours or more.

2. Take banana out of the freezer and stick it in the blender. Get banana out of freezer for about 5 minutes or so prior to making so it won't make the blender work too hard.

3. Add the nut butter and vanilla.

4. Blend until smooth and creamy like ice cream (takes just a minute).

5. Pour in a bowl and enjoy.

Options for Either Alternative

- Replace the vanilla with nutmeg and this is really delightful.

- Cinnamon alone or with nutmeg can be added for a holiday festivity, and even a little pumpkin, if desired.

- Mint extract could be added for a cool, minty, and refreshing taste.

- Orange, cherry, or lemon extract could replace vanilla.

- Chia seeds or chopped sunflower seeds could be sprinkled on top.

- Sunflower butter or chestnut puree could replace typical nut butters.

Pistachio "Ice Cream"

INGREDIENTS

1 medium frozen banana

⅛ tsp vanilla extract

1 or 2 tbsp pistachio butter
(or chopped pistachios if you
have no easy access to butter)

Instructions

1. Get banana out of freezer for about 5 minutes or so prior to making so it won't make the blender work too hard.

2. Put all the ingredients in a blender or food processor and blend for a minute or so. Until it is a nice smooth and creamy consistency.

3. Put in a dish and delight.

Bananacicle

INGREDIENTS

1 medium ripe banana

Instructions

1. Take a banana out of its skin and wrap it in foil or plastic wrap.

2. Stick it in the freezer and freeze for more than 24 hours. Will keep for a couple months.

3. Take out and eat whenever you like.

4. Good as a popsicle alternative on a hot summer's day.

Options

- Could coat with crushed nuts before freezing.

- Dip in melted carob before freezing (please see note on carob on page 54).

- Keep several frozen bananas in the freezer during the summer, so you have them on hand when needed.

"Ice Cream" Bites

INGREDIENTS

Whipped cream from page 137
or dairy-free whipped cream
from page 135

Instructions

1. Place bite size servings of whipped cream into mini cupcake liners.

2. Place liners on a plate.

3. Stick the plate in the freezer until frozen.

4. Once frozen, transfer bites from liners into a freezer baggie for storage in the freezer and eat when desired.

5. Bites made from real deal whipped cream contain about .04 grams per bite if about the size of a tablespoon. Bites made from dairy-free whipped cream contain about 1 gram per bite if tablespoon size. So both can be enjoyed even if you are staying under 50 grams of carbs per day.

Alternative Method

- If you don't have the time, or don't feel like messing with cupcake liners, you can just stick the whipped cream in a baggie, shape it into a log with your hands once it is in the baggie, and stick the baggie in the freezer. Then you can pull it out and cut off a piece with a sharp knife anytime you need and slice that piece into bite size pieces. Run the knife under hot water before slicing.

Options

- Could add chopped nuts to the whipped cream before freezing.

- Any spice or flavor you desire could be added to the whip cream before freezing.

- Little pieces of chopped fruit could be added to the whip cream before freezing.

Pumpkin and Pecan Ice Cream

INGREDIENTS

1 cup of heavy cream	2 tbsp of pumpkin puree
1 tsp of organic vanilla	Stevia to taste
2 or 3 tbsp of pecan butter	

Instructions

1. Pour the cream into a stainless steel bowl. (You could use any type of bowl, but the stainless steel helps it chill faster.)

2. Add all the other ingredients and mix with a fork.

3. Cover with a lid.

4. Stick it in the freezer.

5. Pull it out and stir it every 15 or 20 minutes and put it back in for about 2 hours or to desired consistency.

6. If you have an ice cream maker, you could just pour the mixture in there and let it go according to manufacturers instructions.

Options

- If you are completely avoiding dairy, you could use coconut cream instead of dairy cream. Take a can of coconut milk that has been in the refrigerator overnight and open the can. When coconut milk is chilled, the cream separates from the milk. Scoop the cream out. Alternatively, you could just use the coconut milk as it is, but it won't be as low in carb that way. Additionally, you can buy coconut cream in a can (not to be confused with coconut butter) instead of separating it yourself. See resource section for coconut cream.

- You could use any type of fruit you like instead of the pumpkin.

- You could use any type of nut butter you like instead of pecan.

- You could use whole nuts or chopped nuts or nut meal instead of nut butter.

- Use almond butter and mint flavor instead of pumpkin and pecan.

- Total carb content for this dish, if you eat the whole thing yourself, is about 14.5. Now, I must admit, that I found it impossible to only eat a half cup and I often eat the whole blissful thing. But, if you can find the strength, then you could cut that carb number down to 7.25, if you only eat a half cup. However, I only treat myself to something like this once in a while, so there is no harm in an occasional splurge above your normal carb number, as long as it isn't too drastic and this isn't anywhere near drastic. Not only that, as long as your vegetables are all low-carb, then even if you eat the whole bowl, you can still stay below 50 grams for the day. So, if you're looking for something that is low-carb, homemade, cool, and delicious on a hot summer's day, that you can whip up quickly with no fuss, this will fit the bill.

- Omit nut butter and pumpkin all together and make it plain good old-fashioned vanilla ice cream and the carb content would drop to only 8 if you eat the whole thing and 4 if you cut it in half.

Frozen Fruit Bowl

INGREDIENTS

½ cup of fruit of any kind
(e.g. peaches, strawberries,
blueberries, raspberries, cherries,
bananas, and blackberries)

Instructions

1. Freeze your fruit of choice at least overnight or longer.

2. Take them out and put them in a bowl.

3. You could do just a bowl of berries or just a bowl of peaches or you can mix several of them together.

Options

- You can leave them in whole pieces or you can crush them into a sorbet with your blender. Add a half cup or so of coconut milk or heavy cream with them in the blender to make a mock ice cream.

- Great in the dog days of summer.

- Could put them in a cup of full-fat yogurt for an occasional treat whole, or blend the whole thing together in the blender.

Vanilla Pudding

Yogurt is not a true paleo food and it contains lactose, which means it can feed candida, increase blood glucose, prompt insulin release, and incite cravings for sugar and carbs, etc., and may be problematic for someone with SIBO if overgrowth involves friendly bacteria. Therefore, it is not something that should be eaten daily, but it can be a sensible indulgence now and then, if it does not sabotage your dietary efforts for you.

Like all dairy foods, it can be problematic for those who are vulnerable to the naturally occurring opiates (exorphins) that can provoke neurological symptoms in some people. Naturally, if you fall under this category, this recipe would be avoided.

When you indulge in yogurt, it should always be full-fat to reduce its glycemic index. You may want to choose Greek, because it is lower in lactose and higher in protein than other types.

INGREDIENTS

½ cup full-fat yogurt	Dash of stevia
2 tbsp of macadamia butter	1 vanilla bean

Instructions

1. Put yogurt in a bowl and add the macadamia butter.

2. Slice a vanilla bean in half lengthwise with a sharp knife, then scrape the middle of it with the back of your knife to remove the seeds and sprinkle into your bowl.

3. Stir with a fork until creamy, just 30 seconds or so.

4. You can eat this immediately and it will be like eating pudding. Alternatively, you can chill it in the freezer for an hour or so for a colder treat that resembles ice cream.

5. Great on a hot summer's day.

Options

- Macadamia butter can be replaced with any other nut butter you prefer. However, macadamia is best because it makes it very rich and creamy, just like pudding or ice cream.

- Coconut based yogurt could replace the yogurt.

- Vanilla could be replaced or combined with cinnamon and/or nutmeg. Nutmeg is a very refreshing and delicious option.

- Could throw in a few chia seeds.

Carob Cream

INGREDIENTS

1 8-oz container of heavy cream

1 or 2 tbsp unsweetened carob powder—can adjust for your desired level of carob taste (please see note on carob on page 54 and the resource section)

1 cherry or strawberry

1 tsp of vanilla

Dash of stevia

Instructions

1. Chill a stainless steel bowl in the freezer for a half hour.

2. Put the carob powder, vanilla, and stevia in the bowl with just a little of the heavy cream and stir with a fork or hand whisk to dissolve the powder and remove any clumps.

3. Pour the rest of the cream in the bowl.

4. Mix with mixer until it forms firm peaks (about 4 minute or so).

5. Chill.

6. When ready to serve, put desired amount in a small bowl.

7. Top with cherry or strawberry.

8. Carb content is around 8 so this can be enjoyed even if you are staying below 50 grams of carbs per day.

Any Occasion Fudge

As mentioned previously, carob is not a Paleo for Candida approved food because it is a legume and moderately high in carbs. However, a little carob eaten in moderation a few times a year will not be harmful and is always preferred over chocolate. Therefore, I include this recipe just so you have an alternative to chocolate on holidays and special occasions, like Easter, Valentine's Day, Christmas, etc. Just be sure to reserve this recipe for those special times and don't indulge too frequently. Please see notes on carob on page 54 and on chocolate on page 41.

INGREDIENTS

¼ cup unsweetened carob chips (see resource section)

1 ½ tbsp of your favorite nut butter: almond, macadamia, pecan, cashew, walnut, pistachio (I really like this recipe best with macadamia butter, but they all taste good)

1 tbsp shredded coconut

⅛ cup of water

2 regular sized muffin liners

Dash of stevia

Instructions

1. Put the carob chips in a small sauce pan and cover with the water. You'll need to play around with this a few times to find the right amount of water that produces the consistency you prefer in the fudge. If you like it thin, then a little more water can be used. If you like it really thick, then less water would be used. Taste and texture can be completely different depending on how much water you use. If you end up with something too watery at first, then you can just throw in a few more carob chips.

2. Take it off the stove once it is melted.

3. Stir in the nut butter and stevia. Again, you may want to play around with the amount used to produce the preferred consistency. This recipe is more an art than a science.

4. Divide the mixture evenly between the two muffin liners and sprinkle each one with a little shredded coconut.

5. Stick it in the freezer for about an hour so, until it hardens.

6. Take it out and enjoy.

7. Can store in the freezer overnight and will be just as delicious the next day. It will also keep well for a couple weeks in the freezer.

Options

- Carob powder (see resource section) could be used instead of carob chips. Make a creamy paste by mixing powder and water together in a small sauce pan and cooking for a few minutes.

- This recipe produces a personal size serving. If you want to make it for the entire family, then just increase everything as much as needed.

- Instead of sticking in the freezer or fridge, this could be eaten warm or at room temperature, for a softer fudge.

- Stir in a few raisins before freezing.

- Cinnamon, vanilla, peppermint, or orange flavoring could be added to the carob mixture before freezing.

- You can make a variety of different consistencies by varying the amount of nut butter you add and the amount of water used to melt the carob chips. Different consistencies provide a variety of different textures and flavors. You may find you like it thick or thin or alternate between the two.

- Sunflower butter could be used instead of nut butter.

- Could garnish with a few chia seeds.

- Use a small plate instead of the muffin liners to put the mixture in and this will make a candy bar instead of a fudge. Or it could be poured into candy bar molds.

- On Valentine's Day, you could make the fudge into the shape of a heart. At Christmas and Easter, you can use cookie cutters or candy molds as the mold to pour it in before freezing. Plus you can decorate them with shredded coconut, dried cranberries, raisins, chopped nuts, etc.

Basic Crust

*This makes a very large pie crust or perhaps even
two regular sized crusts, depending on whether
you want side crust or not. If you want a sweeter
crust for a dessert pie, add stevia to taste.*

INGREDIENTS

1 cup coconut flour (3.5 oz)

¼ tsp salt

½ cup solid, cold coconut oil

2 eggs, room temperature

Instructions

1. Preheat the oven to 350.

2. Add coconut flour to a large bowl.

3. Add in the coconut oil and, using a butter knife, cut it into the coconut flour until it becomes small pieces.

4. In a separate bowl, beat 2 eggs until frothy.

5. Slowly add the dry ingredients to the eggs and mix until it becomes smooth and malleable, using your hands if easier.

6. Using a paper towel, spread a small amount of melted coconut oil over the bottom of your pie plate to prevent it from sticking.

7. Press the dough into the pie plate, aiming for an even thickness throughout. Using a fork, pierce the dough every inch. **TIP:** If you don't want the edges to brown, cover them with aluminum foil.

8. Bake for 15 minutes.

9. Alternatively, fill with preferred filling and bake accordingly.

10. This crust can be used for making pies of any kind, chicken pot pies, quiche, or any other recipe that requires a crust.

Classic Apple Pie

INGREDIENTS

Crust from page 174

5 or 6 apples peeled and sliced

1 tsp cinnamon

2 tbsp of water

Dash of salt and stevia

Instructions

1. Combine sliced apples, cinnamon, water, salt, and stevia in a bowl and mix to coat apples thoroughly.

2. Preheat oven to 350.

3. Make two crusts from the recipe on page 174, but don't bake them.

4. Place one crust into 9-inch pie pan as instructed in the crust recipe.

5. Pour apple mixture into the pan on top of the crust.

6. Place the other crust over the top of the apples. This crust does not roll out like crust made with wheat, so you will simply spread it out on the countertop into shape with your fingers as best you can and then lay it on top of the apples. You may need to lay it on top of the apples in numerous smaller pieces, rather than in one large circle. Alternatively, you can just sprinkle the crust across the top in clumps.

7. Bake for about 60 minutes.

8. Let cool for 15 minutes before serving.

Options

● Top with whipped cream from page 135 or 137.

All Purpose Carrot Cake

Please note that cake, even this kind, is not something that should be eaten on a regular basis. This recipe is included so that you have something that will not be too detrimental to your health to use for birthdays and other special occasions.

INGREDIENTS

½ cup melted coconut oil, cooled slightly

6 large eggs, room temperature

1 cup freshly grated carrot (approximately 2 medium sized carrots)

1 cup coconut flour (3.5 oz)

2 tsp baking powder

1 tsp baking soda

2 tbsp vanilla

⅛ to ¼ cup stevia powder to taste

½ to ¾ cup room temperature water

3 tsp ground cinnamon

3 tablespoons raisins

⅓ cup minced walnuts

Dash of salt

3 tbsp freshly squeezed lemon juice

½ cup arrowroot flour/starch

1½ tsp ground allspice

3 tbsp unsweetened coconut flakes

1½ tsp ground ginger

1½ tsp grated nutmeg

½ cup tapioca flour/starch

Instructions

1. Line a square 8 x 8 baking dish with parchment paper, leaving corners extended (this makes removing the loaf from the pan easy).

2. Preheat oven to 350.

3. Combine all the dry ingredients (except for the arrowroot flour, carrot, raisins, walnuts, and coconut flakes) into a large bowl, crushing any lumps and making sure the blend is well combined. Make a well in the center.

4. In a medium sized bowl, using a mixer or by hand, beat eggs until frothy. Add in vanilla and coconut oil.

5. In a small bowl, add the arrowroot flour and gradually add in $1/2$ to $3/4$ cup of room temperature water until the arrowroot is completely wet and the mixture is smooth.

6. Pour half of the egg mixture into the well of the dry ingredients and, by hand, begin to blend. Add in the remaining egg mixture and blend well.

7. Now pour in the arrowroot flour and water mixture and stir a few times.

8. Add in the 3 tablespoons of lemon juice and mix.

9. The mixture will seem very wet and lumpy—keep mixing. This may take a few minutes. Don't forget to scrape along the bottom to incorporate all the dry ingredients but do not over mix. Once the mixture is thick, smooth, and there are no dry lumps, the mixing is complete.

10. Gently fold in carrot, raisins, walnuts, and coconut flakes only until mixed throughout. TIP: If your raisins seem dry, add them to the wet ingredients and let it sit for a few minutes before mixing in the dry ingredients.

11. Spoon the batter into the lined pan and smooth the top. If you do not plan on frosting the cake but want a little extra yumminess, sprinkle the top with some extra coconut flakes and/or finely minced walnuts.

12. It's really important to get the cake into the oven as quickly as possible once the dry and wet ingredients have been mixed together. Bake for 40 to 45 minutes or until knife inserted in center comes out clean.

13. Allow to cool on the counter for 20 to 30 minutes.

14. Refrigerate for at least three hours especially if applying frosting.

15. To frost, use frosting on page 180: either frost the top and sides OR slice the cake in half horizontally and frost the center as well as the top and sides. Sprinkle with coconut flakes and finely minced walnuts.

16. This cake is so moist and tasty it can be enjoyed even without frosting.

17. **Freezing:** Suggest freezing individual pieces rather than the entire cake. Allow to thaw on countertop or refrigerator.

Alternative Method

1. Pour mixture into muffin pan with unbleached liners instead of cake pan. This recipe makes 12 nicely sized muffins.

2. Bake muffins for 20 to 30 minutes depending on your oven.

3. Top with frosting on page 180.

Options

- Could omit walnuts if you can't do nuts, and raisins to lower carb content.

- This cake can be used for birthdays or holidays like Easter, Mother's Day, or Christmas.

Easy Bake Cookies

INGREDIENTS

⅔ cup coconut flour
(2 oz by weight)

¼ cup melted coconut oil,
allowed to cool slightly

⅓ cup tapioca flour

⅛ to ¼ cup stevia powder

1 tsp baking soda

2 tablespoons vanilla extract

2 large eggs,
room temperature

Dash of sea salt

½ tsp baking powder

⅓ cup arrowroot powder

2 tablespoons freshly
squeezed lemon juice

¼ cup of water

Instructions

1. Preheat oven to 350.

2. In a mixing bowl, combine coconut flour, tapioca flour, baking soda, stevia to taste, and sea salt. Make a well in the mixture.

3. In a separate bowl, beat the two eggs until frothy.

4. In another bowl combine the coconut oil, vanilla, and lemon juice and stir.

5. Place the arrowroot flour in a small bowl. Slowly add in $1/8$ cup of water, stirring to break clumps and make it smooth. Add in another $1/8$ cup of water and stir until smooth.

6. Add the eggs to the coconut flour mixture and combine by hand.

7. Add the coconut oil, vanilla, and lemon juice to the bowl containing the flour and egg mixture. Mix by hand until smooth.

8. Lastly, add in the arrowroot flour mixture. Mix only until combined—do not overmix.

9. At this point, you could add in lemon zest, orange zest, carob chips or whatever flavor options you might like. But don't overtax. Or leave them plain.

10. Drop large spoonfuls onto a parchment lined baking sheet.

11. Bake for 12 to 15 minutes or until firm.

12. Let cool for 20 minutes on the counter.

13. Refrigerate them and then enjoy.

14. These cookies are best once they have been refrigerated.

Options

- Chopped nuts could be included.

- A teaspoon of cinnamon could be added.

- Lemon or orange extract could replace the vanilla.

- Please note that baking with coconut flour is more of an art than a science. It tends to be rather finicky, so you may have to play around with it to find the ratio that works best.

Cream Cheese Frosting

INGREDIENTS

4 oz of cream cheese

2 tbsp butter soft

1 tsp vanilla

Dash of stevia

¼ cup of chopped walnuts

Instructions

1. Mix all ingredients in a bowl with electric mixer until consistency of frosting develops (just a couple minutes or so).

2. Put icing on top of cake or muffins and garnish with chopped walnuts.

3. Natural food coloring could be used to add some color to the icing. (See resource section.)

4. Only about 7 grams of carbs in the whole recipe, without the walnuts. With the walnuts, it's an additional 4 grams.

5. This frosting tastes great by itself. It doesn't have to be spread on a pastry. You can just put some in a bowl and eat it or throw in some chopped fruit. Pineapple or cherries are particularly tasty.

BEVERAGES AND SMOOTHIES

Please note: smoothies are not something that should be consumed every day or even weekly. In most cases, a smoothie is going to contain a concentrated level of carbs, which should be reserved for special occasions, holidays, or a treat on a hot summer's day. Your meals should be eaten, not drank. A smoothie should be used as an addition to the meal, not a replacement. They can also be used as a replacement for ice cream or other unhealthy treats.

Blueberry Smoothie

INGREDIENTS

1 cup frozen blueberries

½ frozen banana

1 cup full-fat coconut milk

Instructions

1. Put all the ingredients in the blender and blend until desired consistency.

2. You can vary the amount of coconut milk you use to get different consistencies. With the right ratio you get something like a milk shake, or you can thicken a bit, to get something like ice cream.

3. As stated before, coconut milk comes in light and whole varieties. You should use the whole fat version, because it is much richer, creamier, and healthier for you. I prefer Native Forest, which comes in a BPA-free can.

Options

- Could use heavy cream instead of coconut milk.

Strawberry & Coconut Milk Smoothie

INGREDIENTS

10 oz bag of frozen
strawberries

1 cup full-fat coconut milk

¼ cup finely chopped
macadamia nuts

½ tsp of vanilla

Dash of stevia

Instructions

1. Put all the ingredients in the blender and blend until desired consistency. Divide into two servings.

2. You can vary the amount of coconut milk you use to get different consistencies. The coconut milk is so rich, creamy, and flavorful it makes it almost like a milk shake or with the right ratio you can have something that is almost like ice cream.

3. As mentioned before, coconut milk comes in light and whole varieties. You should use the whole fat version, because it is much richer, creamier, and healthier for you. I prefer Native Forest, which comes in a BPA-free can.

Options

- Macadamias could be replaced with any nut or seed your prefer.
- If you wanted to sweeten it up a bit, you could add half a frozen banana.

Peaches & Almond Milk Smoothie

INGREDIENTS

10 oz bag frozen peaches

1 cup of unsweetened almond milk

Dash of stevia

1 tbsp almond butter

1 tsp of vanilla

Instructions

1. Put the peaches in the blender and turn it into a sorbet. (You can adjust the amount of peaches you add to obtain your desired texture—more fruit makes it thicker, less fruit makes it thinner.)

2. Add the remaining ingredients and blend until smooth. Divide into two servings.

3. Be sure to read the ingredients on the almond milk. Many manufacturers add sugar to theirs and you don't want to use one that has sugar added.

Options

- The almond butter could be omitted, but I think it gives it a more pungent almond flavor and more satiation.

- A dash of cinnamon or nutmeg could be added.

- Peaches could be replaced with other type of fruit.

Cucumber Splash

INGREDIENTS

1 medium cucumber   1 pitcher of water

Instructions

1. Wash your cucumber and cut off the ends.

2. Slice it into one half-inch pieces.

3. Fill a pitcher with purified water.

4. Add the slices of cumber to the pitcher of water.

5. Stir a bit.

6. Stick the pitcher in the fridge for about an hour.

7. Serve over ice or alone.

Options

- Could add a dash of lime juice as well for a change.

- If you just want to make one glass, instead of a whole pitcher, then just add a few slices of cucumber to your glass of water and chill before drinking.

Basic Green Smoothie

INGREDIENTS

1 cup chilled almond milk   ½ avocado

1 cup chopped kale   ½ banana frozen

Instructions

1. Put all the ingredients in the blender and puree.

'Tis the Season Smoothie

INGREDIENTS

1 cup full-fat coconut milk

1 frozen banana

¼ cup chopped pecans

½ tsp pumpkin pie spice mix
(nutmeg, ginger, pumpkin)

Instructions

1. Put all the ingredients in the blender and puree.

Options

● Could use heavy cream instead of coconut milk.

Sparkling Lemonade

INGREDIENTS

1 cup of sparkling mineral water

¼ cup of lemon juice

Instructions

1. Pour sparkling mineral water into a glass.

2. Add lemon juice and stir a tad.

3. It is delightfully refreshing on a hot summer's day.

Options

● Could add a dash of stevia, if you'd like a sweeter drink.

Holiday Nog

*I must admit, one of my favorite activities during the
holidays is my annual glass of eggnog on Christmas Eve
and/or Christmas Day, preferably while I'm watching the
movie* A Christmas Story. *I love eggnog. There's nothing
quite like its thick, rich, and creamy texture and flavor.
Following a low-carb paleo diet does not mean that you
have to forgo these types of beloved holiday traditions.
Not something you should eat daily, but once a year is fine.*

*However, if you buy the traditional store bought option,
then it will be loaded with sugar and other undesirables.
Even the organic brands are loaded with sugar. With just a little
creativity and tweaking in your own kitchen, you can create
this homemade eggnog recipe that is scrumptious and healthy.*

INGREDIENTS

½ cup whole milk

1 cup heavy cream

5 egg yolks

1 tsp nutmeg

½ tsp cinnamon

¼ tsp vanilla

Stevia to taste

½ cup full-fat Greek yogurt

Instructions

1. Put cream, milk, and egg yolks in a blender for about 1 minute.

2. Add stevia, cinnamon, vanilla, and nutmeg and pulse a few times.

3. Chill and serve.

4. Not only is this favorite holiday treat delicious, but its good for you as well. Eggnog is a rich source of fat, protein, and calories, which is good news for those of us following a low-carb or ketogenic diet.

5. After you remove the sugar and alcohol, as we do here, then there really is no reason to feel guilty for indulging in this time honored tradition. So enjoy!

Herbal Iced Tea

The greatest thing about herbal iced tea is that the choices are just about endless, so you can create a different one for every day of the week if you like. You can pick any herbal tea that you enjoy (as long as it doesn't contain caffeine, ferments, or sugar) and turn it into a cool and refreshing beverage.

Some popular choices include lemon, peppermint, spearmint, raspberry, and peach, but be creative and adventurous and try different combinations.

INGREDIENTS

Herbal tea of choice   Water   Dash of stevia (optional)

By the Glass

1. Boil water.

2. Put 2 tea bags in a cup.

3. Pour the water in the cup over your herbs.

4. Steep to desired flavor, may want it to be a little stronger, as flavor may get weaker when chilled.

5. Let it cool.

6. Add a dash of stevia, if you wish.

7. Fill a tall drinking glass with a half cup of ice cubes.

8. Pour the tea over the ice cubes.

By the Pitcher

1. Alternatively could make a whole pitcher.

2. Boil water.

3. Put tea bags in pan of water.

4. Steep for 20 minutes or so.

5. Fill a pitcher half way with ice cubes and pour the tea over it.

6. Alternatively, you can stick the pitcher of tea in the fridge for the day or overnight.

Carb Charts

any low-carb counters use net carbs (total carbs minus fiber content) rather than total carbs when counting their carbs, because they believe that fiber is not absorbed, and therefore, does not increase blood sugar or prompt an insulin response and calories cannot be obtained from it. However, the science on this issue is muddy. This may be true of insoluble fiber, but calories can be obtained from soluble fiber and its impact on blood sugar is not clear. Soluble fiber can be used in gluconeogenesis, which means it could affect blood sugar and the glucose load. It may also disrupt ketosis. Additionally, if you have SIBO or overgrowth of a fiber loving microbe in the colon, then this fiber will serve as a food for source for them. Therefore, I feel it is best to count total carbs, and all the numbers in the following charts will be represented by total carbs, not net carbs.

Total Carbs in Fruit

All data below refers to raw fruit, since that is the way most fruit is consumed. However, if you cook your fruit to make it less offensive for SIBO, then please be aware that one cup of cooked fruit will be higher in carbs than a cup of raw fruit, because in order to get a cup of cooked fruit, there was more raw fruit needed due to loss of water. In other words, more fruit is condensed into one cup. On the other hand, if you bake one apple or pear, or 1 cup of a particular fruit, then the carb content will be the same as it would be if it were raw.

Remember that fruit consumption should be kept to a minimum. Although fruit can be nutritious in moderation, in excess, it can be just as unhealthy as a candy bar and contribute not only to overgrowth of candida and other pathogens, but cravings for sugar and carbs, compulsive overeating, adrenal fatigue, sympathetic nervous system dominance, anxiety, depression, insulin resistance, type 2 diabetes, heart disease, obesity and more. When indulging, stick with low-sugar fruits the majority of the time and use high-sugar fruits for special treats or to satisfy an overwhelming craving for sugar or carbs. Keep serving size to a half cup or smaller. In some cases, consumption may need to be kept to just a few pieces.

All dried fruit is exceptionally high in sugar, so it is typically avoided except on special occasions or to be used when overwhelming cravings for sugar and carbs arise in place of sugar and junk food. However, just a few raisins or date pieces, instead of a cup, could be added to a dish for a little extra flavor on occasion.

Additionally, it's also important to consider the nutritional content of the fruits you consume. Some are higher than others, and ideally, you want to choose those that will give you the most bang for your buck. For example, berries are a rich source of antioxidants and so are cherries, apples, plums, peaches, and pears to a slightly lesser degree.

Fruit juice of any kind should be completely avoided as it is a concentrated source of sugar.

TOTAL CARBS IN RAW FRUIT		
Food	Total Carbs	Serving Size
Apple	25 grams	1 medium
Apricots	3.9 grams	1 whole
Avocado[1]	17 grams	1 average
Banana[2]	27 grams	1 medium
Blackberries	14 grams	1 cup
Blueberries	21 grams	1 cup
Cantaloupe[3]	6 grams	1 wedge ($1/_8$ of medium melon)
Cherries	19 grams	1 cup
Coconut	12 grams	1 cup shredded
Cranberries	12 grams	1 cup
Dates	110 grams	1 cup chopped
Figs Dried	95 grams	1 cup
Figs Fresh (not dried)	12 grams	1 large

Grapefruit	13 grams	1 half
Grapes	16 grams	1 cup
Honeydew melon*3	15 grams	$1/8$ of medium melon
Kiwi	10 grams	1 whole
Lemon	5 grams	1 average
Lime	7 grams	1 whole
Mangos	50 grams	1 mango
Olives*4	0.5 grams	1 jumbo
Orange	11 grams	1 small
Peach	14 grams	1 medium
Pear	27 grams	1 medium
Pineapples	22 grams	1 cup
Plantains	48 grams	1 cup slices
Plum	8 grams	1 plum
Pomegranate	53 grams	1 whole
Raisins	115 grams	1 cup not packed
Raspberries	15 grams	1 cup
Strawberries	11 grams	1 cup whole
Tomato Red*5	4.8 grams	1 medium
Tomato Cherry	6 grams	1 cup
Tomato Sauce	16 grams	1 cup
Watermelon	22 grams	$1/16$ of melon

(Source 1 and 2)

*1. Yes, avocado is a fruit.

*2. The riper the banana, the more sugar it contains, but unripe bananas are high in resistant starch, which feeds SIBO.

*3. Melons are high in mold.

*4. Yes, olive is a fruit.

*5. Yes, tomato is a fruit.

Total Carbs in Vegetables

All numbers below refer to vegetables that are cooked (unless otherwise noted), since I have suggested that people with candida and related conditions like adrenal fatigue, SIBO, etc. do best by consuming cooked food the majority of the time. If you replace a cup of cooked vegetable with a cup of raw vegetables, please note that the carb content would be lower, because more vegetables are condensed into a cup of cooked vegetables than a cup of raw. And as noted in the fruit chart, these are total carbs, not net carbs, for the reasons already discussed on page 189.

TOTAL CARBS IN COOKED VEGETABLES		
Food	Total Carbs	Serving Size
Acorn squash	22 grams	1 cup mashed
Alfalfa sprouts	0.7 grams	1 cup raw
Artichokes	14 grams	1 medium
Asparagus	7.4 grams	1 cup
Beets	16 grams	1 cup
Bok Choy	3 grams	1 cup
Broccoli	12 grams	1 cup
Brussels sprouts	12 grams	1 cup
Butternut squash	22 grams	1 cup cubed
Carrot	12 grams	1 cup slices
Cauliflower	5 grams	1 cup of 1 inch pieces
Celery	1.2 grams	1 stalk raw
Celery	6 grams	1 cup cooked
Collards	11 grams	1 cup
Cucumber	11 grams	1 average raw
Eggplant	9 grams	1 cup
Garlic	3 grams	3 cloves raw
Green beans	10 grams	1 cup

Green bell peppers	9 grams	1 cup chopped or strips
Green cabbage	8.2 grams	1 cup
Green onion/scallion	1.8 grams	1 large raw
Jicama	9 grams	100 grams
Kale	7 grams	1 cup
Leeks	9 grams	1 leek
Lettuce	1 gram	1 cup raw
Mustard greens	6 grams	1 cup
Okra	7.2 grams	1 cup
Onion	10 grams	1 medium
Parsnips	26 grams	1 cup
Potato	37 grams	1 medium baked
Pumpkin	12 grams	1 cup mashed
Radishes	0.2 grams	1 medium raw
Red cabbage	10 grams	1 cup shredded
Rutabagas	12 grams	1 cup
Spaghetti squash	10 grams	1 cup
Spinach	7 grams	1 cup
Summer squash	7 grams	1 cup yellow
Sweet potato	24 grams	1 medium baked
Sweet red bell pepper	12 grams	1 cup chopped
Swiss chard	7 grams	1 cup
Turnips	8 grams	1 cup
Yam	37 grams	1 cup cubed
Zucchini	4.8 grams	1 cup

Note: If you're looking for avocados, olives, and tomatoes, they are technically fruits, so they can be found in the fruit chart on pages 190–191.

(References 1 and 2)

Total Carbs, MUFA, and PUFA in Nuts and Seeds

All data below refers to nuts and seeds that are in their raw and whole state, except for the chestnuts, which are roasted.

1 oz (about 23) Almonds = Carbs 6 grams—MUFA 9 grams—PUFA 3.4 grams, of which 3378 mg is omega-6

1 oz (about 6) Brazil nuts = Carbs 3.5 grams—MUFA 7 grams—PUFA 6 grams, of which 5758 mg is omega-6

1 oz (about 18) Cashews = Carbs 9 grams—MUFA 7 grams—PUFA 2.2 grams, of which 2179 mg is omega-6

1 oz (about 3) roasted Chestnuts = Carbs 15 grams—MUFA 0.2 grams—PUFA 0.2 grams, of which 217 mg is omega-6

1 oz (about 21) Hazelnuts = Carbs 4.7 grams—MUFA 13 grams—PUFA 2.2 grams, of which 2193 mg is omega-6

1 oz (about 10–12) Macadamia nuts = Carbs 3.9 grams—MUFA 17 grams—PUFA 0.4 grams, of which 363 mg is omega-6

1 oz (about 19 halves) Pecans = Carbs 3.9—MUFA 12 grams—PUFA 6 grams, of which 5777 mg is omega-6

1 oz (about 166) Pine nuts = Carbs 3.7 grams—MUFA 5 grams—PUFA 10 grams, of which 9410 mg is omega-6

1 oz (about 49) Pistachios = Carbs 8 grams—MUFA 7 grams—PUFA 3.9 grams, of which 3696 mg is omega-6)

1 oz (about 14 halves) Walnuts = Carbs 3.9 grams—MUFA 2.5 grams—PUFA 13 grams, of which 10666 mg is omega-6)

Seeds

1 oz Chia seeds = Carbs 12 grams—MUFA 0.7 grams—
PUFA 7 grams, of which 1620 omega-6

1 oz Flax seed = Carbs 8 grams—MUFA 2.1 grams—
PUFA 8.00 grams, of which 1655 mg is omega 6

1 oz Hemp seed = Carbs 2 grams—MUFA 0—PUFA 0

1 oz Pumpkin seeds = Carbs 3 grams—MUFA 4.6 grams—
PUFA 6 grams, of which 5797 mg is omega-6

1 oz Sesame seeds = Carbs 7 grams—MUFA 5.3 grams—
PUFA 6.1 grams, of which 5984 mg is omega-6

1 oz Sunflower Seeds= Carbs 6 grams—MUFA 5.2 grams—
PUFA 6.5 grams, of which 6454 mg is omega-6

(References 1 and 2)

Resources

You may be able to find other brands that meet your needs, but these are the brands that I prefer.

Organic Chestnuts Already Roasted in Foil Pouch

Gefen

Season Brand

Organic Grass-fed, Cage-free, Hormone-free, Antibiotic-free Beef and Bison, Poultry, Wild Game, and Seafood

US Wellness Meats (also known as Grassland Beef) http://grasslandbeef.com/

Blackwing https://www.blackwing.com/

Mary's Organic Chicken

Applegate Farms, US Wellness Meats, and Blackwing all carry nitrate free sausage and hot dogs. However, do be cautious of other ingredients that may be present that can increase glutamate or histamine.

Paleo Bread™

Julian Bakery found at www.paleobread.com

Organic Nuts, Seeds, Nut Butters and Seed Butters (Already soaked)

Blue Mountain Organics http://www.bluemountainorganics.com/store/index.htm

Organic Almond Meal (not to be confused with almond flour)

Blue Mountain Organics http://www.bluemountainorganics.com/store/index.htm

Grass-fed Beef Jerky (free of preservatives, sugar, other sweeteners and undesirable ingredients)

US Wellness Meats

There are many brands of paleo jerky on the market, but most of them contain pineapple juice, apple juice, and a lot of spices that can be problems for people with excess glutamate or histamine or autoimmune disorders.

Unsweetened Carob Chips or Powder

Sunspire Carob Chips (not organic, but no sweetener)

Earth Circle (organic unsweetened carob powder)

Swanson (organic unsweetened carob powder)

Organic Pumpkin Puree (BPA Free Can)

Farmers Market

Organic Cage-Free Eggs

Organic Valley

Organic Grass-fed Butter and Heavy Cream

Organic Valley

Natural Food Coloring

India Tree (Nature's Colors Decorating Set)

Frozen Organic Fruits

Woodstock

Cascadian Farm

Whole Foods

Organic Coconut Milk and Coconut Cream

Native Forest (BPA Free Can)

Please note that coconut cream should not be confused with coconut oil or coconut butter. Coconut cream comes in a very small can and consists of nothing but the cream separated from the coconut. Coconut butter is the whole coconut made into a cream and typically comes in a jar like nut butter. Coconut oil is the oil extracted from the coconut and typically comes in a jar as well. Read the label and be sure to distinguish between cream, oil, and butter.

Organic Coconut Butter

Artisana

Nutiva

Again, please note that coconut butter should not be confused with coconut oil or coconut cream. Coconut cream comes in a very small can and consists of nothing but the cream separated from the coconut. Coconut cream is the whole coconut made into a cream and typically comes in a jar like nut butter. Coconut oil is the oil extracted from the coconut and typically comes in a jar as well. Coconut butter is sometimes referred to as Coconut Manna or Creamed Coconut. Read the label and be sure to distinguish between cream, oil, and butter.

Salt

Real Salt

Mixed Bell Peppers (Bag Frozen)

Woodstock Organics

Whole Foods Brand

Organic Virgin Olive Oil

Braggs

Spectrum Naturals

Organic Apple Cider Vinegar

Braggs

Wild Alaskan Salmon

Vital Choice

California Blend Vegetables

Cascadian Farm, Earthbound, Whole Foods, Cadia, and Vons/ Safeway all carry a vegetable blend called California Blend.

Unbleached Muffin Liners and Parchment Paper

If You Care

Paleo Meal Delivery

Paleo on the Go • http://www.paleoonthego.com/

Pete's Paleo • https://petespaleo.com/

Trifecta Nutrition (Associated with Dr. Loren Cordain) • http://trifectanutrition.com/paleo -meal-plans/

Premade Paleo • http://premadepaleo.com/

Mod Paleo • https://store.modpaleo.com/

Database for Restaurants with Paleo Options

paleobytes.com

References

Paleo for Candida Breakfast Ideas

1. Al Sears. "Drop Weight by Eating This at Breakfast" http://www.alsearsmd.com/drop-weight-by-eating-this-at-breakfast/

Nora T. Gedgaudas, *Primal Body Primal Mind: Beyond the Paleo Diet for Total Health and a Longer Life.* (Rochester, VT: Healing Arts Press, 2011).

Loren Cordain. *The Paleo Diet: Lose Weight and Get Healthy by Eating the Foods You Were Designed to Eat.* (Hoboken, NJ: Wiley, 2001).

Al Sears. "It's Not Organic, but so What" http://www.alsearsmd.com/it-is-not-organic-but-so-what/

Tips for Staying on Track

1. Theresa O'Rourke. "The Food Porn Problem." *Women's Health.* August 6, 2012. http://www.womenshealthmag.com/food/food-porn

2. Mark Sisson. *The Primal Blueprint: Reprogram Your Genes for Effortless Weight Loss, Vibrant Health and Boundless Energy.* (Malibu, CA: Primal Nutrition Inc., 2012).

Gauging Carb Intake

1. Jeff Volek and Stephen Phinney. *The Art and Science of Low Carbohydrate Living.* (Beyond Obesity, LLC, 2011).

2. Norman Hord. "Excess omega-3 fatty acids could lead to negative health effects." Oregon State University. http://oregonstate.edu/ua/ncs/archives/2013/oct/excess-omega-3-fatty-acids-could-lead-negative-health-effects

3. Fleishman-Hillard, Inc. "Pistachio consumption may promote a beneficial gut environment." EurekaAlert, April 24, 2012. http://www.eurekalert.org/pub_releases/2012-04/fi-pcm042412.php

4. Jeff Volek and Stephen Phinney. *The Art and Science of Low Carbohydrate Living*. Beyond Obesity, LLC. May 2011.

5. lbid.

6. Mark Sisson. "A Primal Primer: Stevia." http://www.marksdailyapple .com /stevia/#axzz4549CTXNt

7. Mike Adams. "Truvia Sweetener a Powerful Pesticide: Scientists Shocked as Fruit Flies Die in Less than a Week from Eating GMO-derived Erythritol." http://www.naturalnews.com/045450_Truvia_erythritol_natural_pesticide .html

8. Marshall Mandell. *It's Not Your Fault You're Fat Diet*. (New York: HarperCollins, 1983).

William Davis. *Wheat Belly: Lose the Wheat, Lose the Weight, and Find Your Path Back to Health*. (Emmaus, PA: Rodale, 2014).

David Perlmutter. *Grain Brain: The Surprising Truth About Wheat, Carbs, and Sugar—Your Brain's Silent Killers*. (New York: Little, Brown and Company, 2013).

Charles Gant. M.D. *End Your Addiction Now*. (Garden City Park, NY: Square One Publishers, 2009).

Joseph Mercola. "New Revelations Support Diet and Exercise to Reverse Leptin Resistance." http://articles.mercola.com/sites/articles/archive/2012/ 10/29/leptin-resistance.aspx

Carb Charts

1. USDA Food Database via Google Search at www.google.com

2. Self Nutrition Data http://nutritiondata.self.com/

Recipes

A special thank you to Mary-Anne Giancola, who helped me perfect the following recipes: Basic Crust, Holiday Nog, Easy Bake Cookies, and All Purpose Carrot Cake.

Mary-Anne Giancola [CanFit][ICF]—Providing common sense, sustainable methods for fat loss and fitness through positive lifestyle changes. http:// www.magnifywellness.ca/

Index

Acidity, 1, 60
Addiction. *See* Cravings and
    addiction
Adrenal fatigue, 42–43, 191
Agriculture revolution, 3
Alcohol, in fermented foods, 42, 43
Alkalinity, 1, 60
Alkaloids, 12
Almond Butter, Cherries Drizzled
    in, 145
Almond Butter, Vanilla, 142–143
Almond Cremes, 156
Almond flour, 42
Almond meal, 195
Almond Milk & Peaches Smoothie,
    182
Animal protein, 5, 18, 62
    See also Specific type of meat
    in ancestral diet, 3
    blood sugar regulation and, 30,
        45
    for breakfast, 14–16
    buying frozen vs. fresh, 8
    cooking methods and, 8, 22
    daily intake/serving size, 2
    glucose, body's conversion into, 3
    high glutamate, 8
    high histamine/tyramine, 7, 8
    leftovers, 7, 8, 15
    meal planning and, 22–23, 64–68
    resources for, 195
    for satisfying cravings, 17, 29
    snacks, 55–56

Apple cider vinegar, 42, 43, 197
Apples
    Baked Apple Slices with
        Chestnuts, 142
    Classic Apple Pie, 174
    Simply Sautéed Fruit, 160
Asparagus, Oven Roasted, 131
Autoimmune disorders, 6
Avocados, 59
    Avocado and Hard-Boiled Egg
        Sandwich, 73
    Basic Green Smoothie, 183
    Beef & Veggie Wraps, 78–79
    Celery Sticks Snackers, 130–131
    Jalapeno and Guacamole Burger,
        80–81
    Refreshing Cucumber and
        Avocado Salad, 120
    Spicy Guacamole, 116

Balsamic vinegar, 42, 43
Bananas
    Bananacicle, 165
    Banana Cream Bites, 139
    Basic Green Smoothie, 183
    Blueberry Smoothie, 180
    Frozen Fruit Bowl, 168
    Nutty Banana Coconut Bites, 140
    Pistachio "Ice Cream," 165
    Strawberry and Banana Split
        Parfait, 153
    Sunflower Dipped Banana Bites,
        140

Tis the Season Smoothie, 184
Vanilla Bean Banana "Ice
    Cream," 163–164
Barbecue Ribs, Mouth Watering, 99
Barbecue Sauce, Cynthia's, 132
Bars, protein/energy, 55
Beans, 10
Bedtime, eating close to, 44–45, 55
Beef
    See also Ground meat; Hot dogs;
        Sausage
    Beef & Veggie Wraps, 78–79
    Beef Stuffed Cabbage Rolls, 103
    Crock Pot Stew, 83
    Easy Minute Steaks with Mixed
        Peppers, 92–93
    Fajita Bowl, 101
    Homemade Jerky, 104–105
    Mouth Watering Barbecue Ribs,
        99
    resources for, 195
    Savory Slow-Cooked Brisket, 80
    Simple Roast with Vegetables, 92
    Simple Steak Salad, 85
Bell peppers. See Peppers, bell
Berries
    Basic Fruit Salad, 152
    Blueberry Smoothie, 180
    Frozen Fruit Bowl, 168
    Mini Blueberry Cheesecakes, 158
    Mixed Berries and Nuts, 143
    Raspberries and Pears, 136
    Raspberry Cobbler, 159
    Strawberries & Cream, 146
    Strawberry & Coconut Milk
        Smoothie, 181
    Strawberry and Banana Split
        Parfait, 153
Beverages, 68
    Basic Green Smoothie, 183
    Blueberry Smoothie, 180
    at breakfast, 15–16
    Cucumber Splash, 183

Herbal Iced Tea, 186
Holiday Nog, 185
Peaches & Almond Milk
    Smoothie, 182
Sparkling Lemonade, 184
Strawberry & Coconut Milk
    Smoothie, 181
Tis the Season Smoothie, 184
Bison
    See also Ground meat
    All the Fixins Bison Burger,
        84–85
    Bison and Cucumber Salad, 112
    Fajita Bowl, 101
    Ground Beef or Bison with Stir
        Fried Cabbage, 87
    resources for, 195
Blood sugar regulation, 30, 44–45,
    60
Blueberries. See Berries
Blue Mountain Organics, 36, 50,
    195
Bone broth, 6, 41
Books, recommended, 20–21
BPA (bisphenol A), 57
Bread
    gluten-free, 57
    Paleo Bread, 195
    replacements for, 59
Breakfast, 14–16
Brisket, Savory Slow-Cooked, 80
Broccoli
    Cream of Broccoli Soup, 125
    Garlic Roasted Broccoli and/or
        Cauliflower, 115
    as replacement for pasta, 59
Brussels Sprouts, Garlic Flavored,
    116–117
Buffalo Roast with Vegetables, 92
Burgers and patties
    All the Fixins Bison Burger,
        84–85
    Basic Bunless Burger, 76

Jalapeno and Guacamole Burger,
    80–81
    Salmon Patties, 81
    Southwestern Turkey Burger, 82
Butter, dairy, 51
    See also Specific recipe
    lactose in, 10
    paleo diet and, 3, 52
    for raising blood sugar levels, 60
    resources for, 196
    Sweet or Spicy Butter Balls,
        132–133
Butter, nondairy, 47, 60
    See also Candies; Macadamia
        butter
    All-Purpose No-Bake Thumbprint
        Cookies, 149–150
    Any Occasion Fudge, 171–172
    Cherries Drizzled in Almond
        Butter, 145
    Nuts and Cream, 159–160
    Nutty Banana Coconut Bites, 140
    oxidation and, 50
    Peaches & Almond Milk
        Smoothie, 182
    Pistachio "Ice Cream," 165
    Pumpkin and Pecan Ice Cream,
        167–168
    Pumpkin Pie Mousse, 151–152
    resources for, 195, 196
    Vanilla Almond Butter, 142–143

Cabbage
    Beef Stuffed Cabbage Rolls, 103
    Broiled Hot Dogs with Fried
        Cabbage, 86–87
    Cabbage in Olive Oil, 117
    Cinnamon Cabbage, 118
    Ground Beef or Bison with Stir
        Fried Cabbage, 87
    Holiday Kraut & Dogs Casserole,
        90–91
    Pasta-Free Lasagna, 108–109

Pasta-Free Spaghetti in Meat
        Sauce; variation, 72
    as replacement for bread/pasta,
        59
    Scrambled Eggs with Cabbage
        and Olives, 91
Caffeine, 15–16, 17, 41
California blend vegetables
    Baked Chicken Breast with, 93
    Pasta-Free Spaghetti in Meat
        Sauce; variation, 72
    resources for, 197
Candida diet. *See* Paleo for Candida
    Diet
Candies
    Almond Cremes, 156
    Cinnamon Drops, 155
    Lemon Drops, 154
    Macadamia Cremes, 155–156
    Maple Leaves, 156
    options and tips for, 157
    Vanilla Drops, 155
Candy, and holidays, 32–38
Canned foods, 12, 57
Cantaloupes, 47
Carbohydrates
    See also Cravings and addiction;
        Fruit; Nuts; Seeds; Vegetables
    avoiding snacking on, 45, 55
    bedtime, eating close to, 44–45
    blood sugar elevation/crash and,
        30
    breakfast and, 14
    candida population, health risks
        for, 1–2
    cinnamon with, 60
    counting charts, by food type,
        188–194
    daily intake of, 2, 44–47
    dessert recipes, low-carb, 44
    fat, combining with, 46
    high-carb paleo approved foods,
        2, 4, 42

as non-essential to human body,
3
SIBO and, 2, 11–12
Carob
All-Purpose No-Bake Thumbprint
Cookies, 149–150
Any Occasion Fudge, 171–172
Carob Cream, 170
overview, 54–55
as replacement for chocolate,
36–37
resources for, 196
Carrot Cake, All Purpose, 175–177
Cashews, 48
Casserole, Holiday Kraut & Dogs,
90–91
Casserole, Zucchini Noodle and
Sausage, 110
Cauliflower
Cauliflower Rice, 113
Garlic Roasted Broccoli and/or
Cauliflower, 115
Mock Mashed Potatoes, 127
as replacement for pasta, 59
Rich and Creamy Cauliflower
Soup, 126
Shepherd's Pie, 77
Celery Soup, Chunky, 124
Celery Sticks Snackers, 130–131
Cheese. *See* Dairy
Cheesecakes, Mini Blueberry, 158
Chemicals, 27, 54
Cherries Drizzled in Almond Butter,
145
Chestnut flour, 42
Chestnuts, 49
Baked Apple Slices with
Chestnuts, 142
Chestnut Puree, 161
Gesztenyepure (Hungarian
Chestnut Puree), 162
overview, 50–51
resources for, 195

Chia seeds, 48–49
Chicken. *See* Poultry
Children, 19
See also Holidays
Chocolate, 17, 41
See also Carob
Christmas. *See* Holidays
Cigarette cravings, triggers for, 12
Cinnamon, 60
Cinnamon Baked Pears with
Pecans, 138
Cinnamon Cabbage, 118
Cinnamon Drops, 155
Citric acid, 12
Citrus fruits, 6, 47
Cobbler, Raspberry, 159
Coconut aminos, 41
Coconut butter, 60, 140, 196
See also Candies
Coconut cream, 196
Coconut flour, 42
Coconut milk
Blueberry Smoothie, 180
Chestnut Puree, 161
Coconut Pops, 162–163
Dairy-Free Whipped Cream,
135–136
resources for, 196
Strawberry & Coconut Milk
Smoothie, 181
Tis the Season Smoothie, 184
Coconut oil, 51, 196
Coffee, 15–16, 41
Complex carbohydrates, 17
Conflict, 31
Cookies
All-Purpose No-Bake Thumbprint
Cookies, 149–150
Easy Bake Cookies, 177–178
Sunflower Macaroons, 144
Cooking methods
gas or propane stoves/ovens, 56
histamines/tyramines and, 8

oxalates and, 9, 59
raw vs. cooked foods, 42–43
SIBO and, 11–12, 43, 59
slow cooking, 8, 22
steaming vs. boiling, 9, 59
teflon or aluminum pans and,
    56–57
Cornish Hen and Vegetables, 107
Cortisol, 45
Cranberry Sauce, Holiday, 133
Cravings and addiction
    breakfast and, 14
    carb intake and, 2, 45–47
    dried fruit for, 59–60, 189
    emotional factors, 27–28, 31
    food porn and, 29
    food sensitivities and, 13
    food triggers, 17–18, 41–42, 43
    handling, tips for, 29
    holidays and, 32–38
    individual factors, 13
    inner voice and, 32
    lifestyle factors, 31–32
    low blood sugar and, 30, 44–45,
        60
    meals, timing of, 30
    mindful eating, 25–27
    mindset, 18, 24–25
    nicotine/cigarettes, 12
    paleo approved foods and, 40
    planning ahead, 22–23
    removing unhealthy foods from
        the house, 18–19
    setbacks and relapses, 38–39
    snacks, 45, 55–56
    spiritual health and, 28–29
    support system, 20–21
    toxins and, 27
    during transition period, 21
Cream (dairy)
    Banana Cream Bites, 139
    Carob Cream, 170
    Holiday Nog, 185

"Ice Cream" Bites, 166
lactose in, 10
Nuts and Cream, 159–160
paleo diet and, 3, 52
Pumpkin and Pecan Ice Cream,
    167–168
Real Deal Whipped Cream, The,
    137
resources for, 196
Spiced Peaches and Cream
    Paradise, 141
Strawberries & Cream, 146
Cream Cheese Frosting, 179
Crock pot dishes. See Slow cooking
Crust, Basic, 173
Crust, Nutty, 148
Crustless Quiche with Sausage and
    Veggies, 98–99
Cucumbers
    Bison and Cucumber Salad, 112
    Cucumber Splash, 183
    Refreshing Cucumber and
        Avocado Salad, 120
    Tangy Cucumbers, 122
Cultured foods, 6, 41, 42
Cynthia's Barbecue Sauce, 132

Dairy, 60
    See also Butter, dairy; Cream;
        Yogurt
    autoimmune disorders and, 6
    Cream Cheese Frosting, 179
    high glutamate, 8
    high histamine/tyramine, 6, 7
    lactose/lactose intolerance and,
        10, 52
    Mini Blueberry Cheesecakes, 158
    paleo diet and, 3, 52–53, 62–63
    Pasta-Free Lasagna, 108–109
    raw, 10
    resources for, 196
Dairy-Free Whipped Cream,
    135–136

Dates, Dipped, 146
Delivery services for paleo meals, 61, 197
Desserts, 42, 47
  See also Candies
  All Purpose Carrot Cake, 175–177
  All-Purpose No-Bake Thumbprint Cookies, 149–150
  Any Occasion Fudge, 171–172
  Baked Apple Slices with Chestnuts, 142
  Banana Bites, 139–140
  Bananacicle, 165
  Basic Crust, 173
  Basic Fruit Salad, 152
  Carob Cream, 170
  Cherries Drizzled in Almond Butter, 145
  Chestnut Puree, 161
  Cinnamon Baked Pears with Pecans, 138
  Classic Apple Pie, 174
  Coconut Pops, 162–163
  Cream Cheese Frosting, 179
  Dairy-Free Whipped Cream, 135–136
  Dipped Dates, 146
  Easy Bake Cookies, 177–178
  Frozen Fruit Bowl, 168
  Gesztenyepure (Hungarian Chestnut Puree), 162
  "Ice Cream" Bites, 166
  Mini Blueberry Cheesecakes, 158
  Mixed Berries and Nuts, 143
  Nuts and Cream, 159–160
  Nutty Crust, 148
  Peach Crumble, 147–148
  Pears and Raspberries, 136
  Pistachio "Ice Cream," 165
  Pumpkin and Pecan Ice Cream, 167–168
  Pumpkin Pie Mousse, 151–152
  Raspberry Cobbler, 159
  Real Deal Whipped Cream, The, 137
  recipes with low-carb content, 44
  sample meal plans, 64–68
  Simply Sautéed Fruit, 160
  Spiced Peaches and Cream Paradise, 141
  Strawberries & Cream, 146
  Strawberry and Banana Split Parfait, 153
  Sunflower Macaroons, 144
  Vanilla Almond Butter, 142–143
  Vanilla Bean Banana "Ice Cream," 163–164
  Vanilla Pudding, 169–170
Diet for candida. *See* Paleo for Candida Diet
Dining out, 60–61, 197
Dressing, Basic, 121
Dried fruits, 59–60, 189
Duck, Simple Roast, 82–83
Duck Breast, Seared, 84

Easter, and diet compliance, 37–38
Easter eggs, dye for coloring, 60
Eating out, 60–61, 197
Eggplants, 12
Eggs, 6, 7
  Avocado and Hard-Boiled Egg Sandwich, 73
  Crustless Quiche with Sausage and Veggies, 98–99
  dye for coloring, at Easter, 60
  Holiday Nog, 185
  Pepper and Spinach Egg Scramble, 88
  Quick and Simple Paleo Omelet, 106
  resources for, 196
  Scrambled Eggs with Cabbage and Olives, 91
Emotional factors, 27–28, 31

Emotional support, 20–21
Environmental toxins, 27, 54
Erythritol, 54
Estrogen. *See* Phytoestrogens
Exercise, 31

Fajita Bowl, 101
Family, 19
   See also Holidays
Fasting, intermittent, 30
Fat, dietary, 5, 18
   See also Butter; Dairy; Ghee;
     Nuts; Seeds
   in ancestral diet, 3
   blood sugar regulation and, 30,
     45, 60
   for breakfast, 14–16
   combining with high-carb foods,
     46
   glucose/ketones, conversion into,
     3
   MUFAs/PUFAs, 48–49, 50, 51,
     193–194
   need for, with low-carb diet, 2,
     52
   oils, 51–52
   for satisfying cravings, 17, 29
   as snack, 55
Fat burner, transition to, 3, 12, 46,
   55
Fermented foods, 6, 7, 41, 42, 43
Fiber, 11–12, 43, 188
Fish
   Baked Salmon in Lemon and
     Garlic Butter, 111
   high histamine/tyramine, 7
   resources for, 197
   Salmon Patties, 81
Flax seeds, 49
Flours, 42
FODMAPs (fructans, galactans,
   lactose, and polyols), 9–11
Food coloring, 60, 196

Food delivery services, 61, 197
Food labels, 57–58
Food porn, 29
Food sensitivities, 13
Foods to eat/avoid, 3–4, 62–63
Food storage containers, 57
FOS supplement, 10
Frosting, Cream Cheese, 179
Frozen vs. fresh foods, 8, 60
Fructans, 10
Fructose, 10–11
Fruit
   See also Desserts; Smoothies
   avoiding snacking on, 45, 55
   candida population, health risks
     for, 41–42
   canned, 57
   carb content, by type, 188–190
   cooked vs. raw, 46, 188
   daily intake/serving size, 2, 46,
     189
   dried, 59–60, 189
   fat, combining with, 46
   frozen vs. fresh, 60
   high FODMAPs, 9–11
   high histamine/tyramine, 6–8
   high oxalate, 9
   minimizing consumption of,
     188–189
   mold and, 47
   resources for, 196
   SIBO and, 11–12, 47, 59, 188
   sugar (fructose) in, 10–11
Fruit juice, 60, 189
Fudge, Any Occasion, 171–172

Galactans, 10
Garlic Flavored Brussels Sprouts,
   116–117
Garlic Roasted Broccoli and/or
   Cauliflower, 115
Gas ovens/stoves, 56
Gelatin, 60

Gesztenyepure (Hungarian Chestnut
Puree), 162
Ghee, 3, 10, 51, 52
Gluconeogenesis, 3, 188
Glucose/fructose ratio, 11
Glucose production, in body, 3
Glutamate foods, high, 8, 12, 22,
41, 42, 43, 60
Glycemic index, lowering, 29, 46,
60
Glyphosate (Roundup), 54
Grains, 3–4, 17, 63
Greek yogurt, 52
Green beans
Crock Pot Stew, 83
Fresh Chicken Salad Medley, 71
Green Beans in Herbs, 122–123
Lemon & Almond Green Bean
Salad, 118–119
Spicy Green Beans and Ground
Beef, 86
Green lifestyle, 27
Green Smoothie, Basic, 183
Ground meat
All the Fixins Bison Burger,
84–85
Basic Bunless Burger, 76
Caveman's Palate Meat Loaf, 89
Ground Beef or Bison with Stir
Fried Cabbage, 87
Jalapeno and Guacamole Burger,
80–81
Meatza Pizza Pie, 74–75
Mexican Paleo Wrap, 94–95
Pasta-Free Lasagna, 108–109
Pasta-Free Spaghetti in Meat
Sauce, 72
Savory Paleo Meat Balls, 102
Shepherd's Pie, 77
Southwestern Turkey Burger, 82
Spicy Green Beans and Ground
Beef, 86
Guacamole, Spicy, 116

Guacamole and Jalapeno Burger,
80–81
Gut health, 1, 12, 31, 48, 49–50,
51

Halloween, 33–35
Hazelnuts, 48
Herb & Lemon Chicken, 78
Herbal Iced Tea, 186
Herb and Mustard Chicken Thighs,
75
Herbed Kale Salad, 119
Herbs, Green Beans in, 122–123
Hereditary fructose intolerance, 11
High-carb foods, paleo approved, 2,
4, 41–42
Histamine or tyramine foods, high,
6–8, 41, 42, 43, 59, 60
Hoagie-less Sausage with Peppers
and Onions, 95
Holidays, 154, 157, 171–172
Christmas, 37–38
Easter, 37–38
Easter eggs, dye for coloring, 60
Halloween, 33–35
Holiday Cranberry Sauce, 133
Holiday Kraut & Dogs Casserole,
90–91
Holiday Nog, 185
overview, 32–33
Pumpkin Pie Mousse, 151–152
Valentine's Day, 35–37
Hot dogs
Broiled Hot Dogs with Fried
Cabbage, 86–87
Holiday Kraut & Dogs Casserole,
90–91
resources for, 195
Hungarian Chestnut Puree
(Gesztenyepure), 162
Hydration, 53, 60

"Ice cream"

"Ice Cream" Bites, 166
Pistachio "Ice Cream," 165
Pumpkin and Pecan Ice Cream, 167–168
Vanilla Bean Banana "Ice Cream," 163–164
Individualized Paleo for Candida Plan, 5
autoimmune disorders, 6
carb intake, 44–47
food sensitivities, 13
high FODMAPs foods, 9–11
high glutamate foods, 8
high histamine or tyramine foods, 6–8
high oxalate foods, 9
nightshade family foods, 12
SIBO and, 11–12
weight management, 12–13, 46
Inner voice, 32
Insulin, 45
Intermittent fasting, 30

Jalapeno and Guacamole Burger, 80–81
Jello, 60
Jerky, Homemade, 104–105
Jerky, resources for, 195
Juice, fruit, 60, 189

Kale, in Basic Green Smoothie, 183
Kale Salad, Herbed, 119
Kefir, 6
Ketogenic diet, 5
Ketones, 3
Kraut & Dogs Casserole, Holiday, 90–91

Labels, food, 57–58
Lactose, 10, 52
Lactose intolerance, 10
Lamb Chops with Herbs, Pan-Roasted, 97

Lamb Roast with Celery, Leg of, 100–101
Lard, 51
Lasagna, Pasta-Free, 108–109
Lectins, 12, 49
Leftovers, 7, 8, 15
Legumes, 4, 10, 17, 36–37, 48, 54
Lemon & Herb Chicken, 78
Lemonade, Sparkling, 184
Lemon Drops, 154
Leptin, 31
Lifestyle factors, 31–32
Low blood sugar, 30, 44–45, 60
Low-carb. See Carbohydrates; Paleo for Candida Diet

Macadamia butter
Any Occasion Fudge, 171–172
Celery Sticks Snackers, 130–131
with Dipped Dates, 146
Macadamia Cremes, 155–156
Vanilla Bean Banana "Ice Cream," 163–164
Vanilla Pudding, 169–170
Macadamia nuts, 48, 49, 50
Macadamia oil, 51
Macaroons, Sunflower, 144
Main dishes
All the Fixins Bison Burger, 84–85
Aromatic Roasted Pheasant with Carrots and Celery, 79
Avocado and Hard-Boiled Egg Sandwich, 73
Baked Chicken Breast with California Blend Vegetables, 93
Baked Chicken Tenders, 70–71
Baked Salmon in Lemon and Garlic Butter, 111
Basic Bunless Burger, 76
Basic Roasted Turkey Breast, 69
Beef & Veggie Wraps, 78–79

Beef Stuffed Cabbage Rolls, 103

Bison and Cucumber Salad, 112

Broiled Hot Dogs with Fried
Cabbage, 86–87

Caveman's Palate Meat Loaf, 89

Chicken Salad Supreme, 94

Cornish Hen and Vegetables, 107

Crock Pot Stew, 83

Crustless Quiche with Sausage
and Veggies, 98–99

Easy Minute Steaks with Mixed
Peppers, 92–93

Fajita Bowl, 101

Fast and Easy Paleo Pizza, 96–97

Fresh Chicken Salad Medley, 71

Ground Beef or Bison with Stir
Fried Cabbage, 87

Hoagie-less Sausage with Peppers
and Onions, 95

Holiday Kraut & Dogs Casserole,
90–91

Homemade Jerky, 104–105

Jalapeno and Guacamole Burger,
80–81

Leg of Lamb Roast with Celery,
100–101

Lemon & Herb Chicken, 78

Meatza Pizza Pie, 74–75

Mexican Paleo Wrap, 94–95

Mouth Watering Barbecue Ribs,
99

Mustard and Herb Chicken
Thighs, 75

Pan-Roasted Lamb Chops with
Herbs, 97

Pasta-Free Lasagna, 108–109

Pasta-Free Spaghetti in Meat
Sauce, 72

Pepper and Spinach Egg
Scramble, 88

Quick and Simple Paleo Omelet,
106

Salmon Patties, 81

Savory Paleo Meat Balls, 102

Savory Slow-Cooked Brisket, 80

Scrambled Eggs with Cabbage
and Olives, 91

Seared Duck Breast, 84

Shepherd's Pie, 77

Simple Roast Duck, 82–83

Simple Roast with Vegetables, 92

Simple Steak Salad, 85

Southwestern Turkey Burger, 82

Spicy Green Beans and Ground
Beef, 86

Turkey Loaf, 90

Zucchini Noodle and Sausage
Casserole, 110

Maple Leaves, 156

Mashed Potatoes, Mock, 127

Meal delivery services, 61, 197

Meals

avoiding skipping, 30

breakfast, 14–16

intermittent fasting, 30

keeping it simple, 23

leftovers, 7, 8, 15

mindful eating during, 25–27

planning ahead for, 22–23

sample plans for, 64–68

snacks, 45, 55–56

timing of, 30

Meat. See Animal protein

Meat Balls, Savory Paleo, 102

Meat Loaf, Caveman's Palate, 89

Meat Loaf, Turkey, 90

Meditation, 28

Melons, 47

Menopause. See Postmenopausal
women

Menu plans, 64–68

Mexican Paleo Wrap, 94–95

Microwave ovens, 57

Migrating motor complex (MMC),
31, 56

Milk, 8, 10

Mindful eating, 25–27
Mindfulness meditation, 28
Mindset, 18, 24–25
Mold, 47, 48, 50
Monounsaturated fats (MUFAs), 48–49, 50, 51, 193–194
Mousse, Pumpkin Pie, 151–152
MUFAs. *See* Monounsaturated fats
Muffin liners, 57, 197
Muffins, All Purpose Carrot Cake, 177
Mustard and Herb Chicken Thighs, 75

Nature, communing with, 32
Nicotine, 12
Nightshade family foods, 12
No-Bake Thumbprint Cookies, All-Purpose, 149–150
Nog, Holiday, 185
Noodle and Sausage Casserole, Zucchini, 110
Noodles, Zucchini, 114–115
Norepinephrine, 45
Nut butter. *See* Butter, nondairy
Nuts, 47–51
    See also Specific nut; recipe
    autoimmune disorders and, 6
    avoiding snacking on, 45, 55
    Baked Apple Slices with Chestnuts, 142
    Banana Cream Bites, 139
    candida population, health risks for, 41–42
    carb content, by type, 193
    Chestnut Puree, 161
    Cinnamon Baked Pears with Pecans, 138
    daily intake/serving size, 2, 46–47
    Gesztenyepure (Hungarian Chestnut Puree), 162
    high glutamate, 8
    high histamine/tyramine, 6, 7

high oxalate, 9
    Mixed Berries and Nuts, 143
    mold and, 48, 50
    MUFAs/PUFAs in, 48–49, 50, 51, 193
    Nuts and Cream, 159–160
    Nutty Crust, 148
    omega-3/omega-6 and, 48–49, 51, 193–194
    overview, 47–51
    oxidation of, 50, 51, 52
    phytates in, 49–50
    raw vs. roasted, 46–47
    resources for, 195
    SIBO and, 11–12, 48, 50, 51
    soaking and roasting, 49–50
    Tis the Season Smoothie, 184

Obesity. *See* Overweight
Oils, 51–52
Olive oil, 7, 52, 197
Olives, 7, 59
Omega-3/omega-6 fatty acids, 48–49, 51, 193–194
Oranges, 47
Ovens, gas/propane, 56
Overweight, 12, 46
Oxalate foods, high, 9, 59
Oxidation, 50, 51, 52

Paleo Bread, 195
Paleo for Candida Diet
    See also Animal protein; Carbohydrates; Cooking methods; Cravings and addiction; Fat, dietary; Small intestinal bacterial overgrowth
    as ancestral diet, 3
    autoimmune disorders and, 6
    blood sugar regulation, 30, 44–45, 60
    breakfast, 14–16
    children/partners and, 19

compared to paleo diets for
general population, 40–43
cooked vs. raw foods, 42–43
food sensitivities, 13
foods to eat/avoid, 3–4, 62–63
high FODMAPs foods, 9–11
high glutamate foods, 8
high histamine or tyramine foods,
6–8
high oxalate foods, 9
individualizing to your needs,
5–13
as lifestyle, 38
meal plans, samples of, 64–68
meals, timing of, 30
mindful eating, 25–27
mindset, 18, 24–25
nightshade foods, 12
overview, 1–4, 62–63
planning meals, 22–23, 64–68
remaining compliant with, tips
for, 17–39
safety of, 3
salt, 53, 60
snacks, 45, 55–56
stevia, 53–54
weight management, 12–13, 46
Paleo meal delivery services, 61, 197
Paleo/primal cookbooks, 40–43
Pans, 56–57
Parchment paper, 57, 197
Partners, 19
Pasta alternatives, 59
Pasta-Free Lasagna, 108–109
Pasta-Free Spaghetti in Meat
Sauce, 72
Zucchini Noodle and Sausage
Casserole, 110
Zucchini Noodles, 114–115
Pastries, 42, 57
Patties. See Burgers and patties
Peaches
Frozen Fruit Bowl, 168

Peach Crumble, 147–148
Peaches & Almond Milk
Smoothie, 182
Simply Sautéed Fruit, 160
Spiced Peaches and Cream
Paradise, 141
Peanuts, 48
Pears
Cinnamon Baked Pears with
Pecans, 138
Pears and Raspberries, 136
Simply Sautéed Fruit, 160
Pecan and Pumpkin Ice Cream,
167–168
Pecans, Cinnamon Baked Pears
with, 138
Pecans, 48
Peppers, bell
Caveman's Palate Meat Loaf, 89
Crustless Quiche with Sausage
and Veggies, 98–99
Easy Minute Steaks with Mixed
Peppers, 92–93
Fast and Easy Paleo Pizza, 96–97
Hoagie-less Sausage with Peppers
and Onions, 95
Pepper and Spinach Egg
Scramble, 88
resources for, 197
Savory Paleo Meat Balls, 102
Zucchini Noodle and Sausage
Casserole, 110
Pesticides, 54
pH (acidity versus alkalinity), 1, 60
Pheasant with Carrots and Celery,
Aromatic Roasted, 79
Physical activity, 31
Phytates (phytic acid), 9, 49–50
Phytoestrogens, 49
Pie, Classic Apple, 174
Pie crust
Basic Crust, 173
Nutty Crust, 148

Pineapple, 47
Pine nuts, 48–49
Pistachio "Ice Cream," 165
Pistachios, 48, 51
Pizza, Fast and Easy Paleo, 96–97
Pizza Pie, Meatza, 74–75
Planning meals, 22–23, 64–68
Polyols, 11
Polyunsaturated fats (PUFAs),
    48–49, 50, 193–194
Pops, Coconut, 162–163
Pork, 43, 51
Positive mindset, 24–25
Postmenopausal women, 12, 46
Potatoes, 4, 17
Potatoes, Mock Mashed, 127
Poultry
    Aromatic Roasted Pheasant with
        Carrots and Celery, 79
    Baked Chicken Breast with
        California Blend Vegetables,
        93
    Baked Chicken Tenders, 70–71
    Basic Roasted Turkey Breast, 69
    Chicken Salad Supreme, 94
    Cornish Hen and Vegetables, 107
    Fajita Bowl, 101
    Fresh Chicken Salad Medley, 71
    high histamine/glutamate, 7, 8
    Homemade Jerky, 104–105
    Lemon & Herb Chicken, 78
    Mustard and Herb Chicken
        Thighs, 75
    resources for, 195
    Seared Duck Breast, 84
    Simple Roast Duck, 82–83
    Southwestern Turkey Burger, 82
    Turkey Loaf, 90
Prebiotics, 51
Preparation of meals. See Cooking
    methods; Meals
Processed foods, 55
Propane ovens/stoves, 56

Protease inhibitors, 49
Protein. See Animal protein
Pudding, Vanilla, 169–170
PUFAs (polyunsaturated fats),
    48–49, 50, 193–194
Pumpkin
    Pumpkin and Pecan Ice Cream,
        167–168
    Pumpkin Pie Mousse, 151–152
    resources for, 196

Quiche with Sausage and Veggies,
    Crustless, 98–99

Raspberries
    Frozen Fruit Bowl, 168
    Raspberries and Pears, 136
    Raspberry Cobbler, 159
Raw dairy, 10
Raw vs. cooked foods, 42–43
Resistant starch, 11–12, 43, 190
Resources, 195–197
Restaurants, 60–61, 197
Ribs, Mouth Watering Barbecue, 99
Rice, Cauliflower, 113
Rolls, Beef Stuffed Cabbage, 103
Roundup (glyphosate), 54

Salads
    Basic Dressing, 121
    Bison and Cucumber Salad, 112
    Chicken Salad Supreme, 94
    Fajita Bowl, 101
    Fresh Chicken Salad Medley, 71
    Herbed Kale Salad, 119
    Lemon & Almond Green Bean
        Salad, 118–119
    Refreshing Cucumber and
        Avocado Salad, 120
    Simple Steak Salad, 85
Salmon. See Fish
Salt, 53, 60
Sample meal plans, 64–68

Sandwich, Avocado and Hard-
Boiled Egg, 73
Saponins, 12
Sauce, Cynthia's Barbecue, 132
Sauce, Holiday Cranberry, 133
Sausage
    Crustless Quiche with Sausage
    and Veggies, 98–99
    Fast and Easy Paleo Pizza, 96–97
    Hoagie-less Sausage with Peppers
    and Onions, 95
    resources for, 195
    Zucchini Noodle and Sausage
    Casserole, 110
Seafood, 7, 8, 195
Seeds, 6, 7, 9
    See also Specific recipe
    avoiding snacking on, 45, 55
    carb content, by type, 194
    mold and, 48, 50
    MUFAs/PUFAs in, 48–49, 50,
    194
    overview, 47–50
    oxidation of, 50
    phytates in, 49–50
    resources for, 195
    soaking and roasting, 49–50
Self-medicating, 31
Sensitivities, food, 13
Shepherd's Pie, 77
SIBO. See Small intestinal bacterial
    overgrowth
Side dishes
    Cabbage in Olive Oil, 117
    Cauliflower Rice, 113
    Celery Sticks Snackers, 130–131
    Cinnamon Cabbage, 118
    Cynthia's Barbecue Sauce, 132
    Garlic Flavored Brussels Sprouts,
    116–117
    Garlic Roasted Broccoli and/or
    Cauliflower, 115
    Green Beans in Herbs, 122–123

    Holiday Cranberry Sauce, 133
    I'm in Nirvana Sweet Potato,
    128–129
    Lemon & Almond Green Bean
    Salad, 118–119
    Mock Mashed Potatoes, 127
    Oven Roasted Asparagus, 131
    Quick and Simple Sautéed
    Spinach, 123
    Roasted Zucchini & Yellow
    Squash, 134
    Spicy Guacamole, 116
    Sweet or Spicy Butter Balls,
    132–133
    Tangy Cucumbers, 122
    Zucchini Noodles, 114–115
Sleep, 31–32, 44–45
Slow cooking
    amines and, 8
    Crock Pot Stew, 83
    glutamate and, 22
    Savory Slow-Cooked Brisket, 80
Small intestinal bacterial overgrowth
    (SIBO), 41, 53, 54
    cooked food and, 11–12, 43, 59
    daily carb intake, 2, 11
    fruit and, 11–12, 47, 59, 188
    intermittent fasting and, 30
    nuts and seeds and, 11–12, 48,
    50, 51
    overview, 11–12
    snacking and, 56
Smoothies
    Basic Green Smoothie, 183
    Blueberry Smoothie, 180
    Peaches & Almond Milk
    Smoothie, 182
    Strawberry & Coconut Milk
    Smoothie, 181
    Tis the Season Smoothie, 184
Snackers, Celery Sticks, 130–131
Snacks, 55–56
    foods to eat/avoid as, 45, 55

options for, 56
sample meal plans, 64–68
Sodium. *See* Salt
Soups
  Chunky Celery Soup, 124
  Cream of Broccoli Soup, 125
  Crock Pot Stew, 83
  Rich and Creamy Cauliflower
    Soup, 126
  Simple Zucchini Soup, 124
Southwestern Turkey Burger, 82
Spaghetti in Meat Sauce, Pasta-Free,
  72
Spaghetti sauce, vegetables with, 59
Sparkling Lemonade, 184
Spiced Peaches and Cream Paradise,
  141
Spices
  See also Cinnamon
  being creative with, 47, 59
  high histamine/glutamate, 7, 8
  reading labels, 57
Spicy Green Beans and Ground Beef,
  86
Spicy Guacamole, 116
Spicy or Sweet Butter Balls, 132–133
Spinach
  Caveman's Palate Meat Loaf, 89
  Crustless Quiche with Sausage
    and Veggies, 98–99
  Pepper and Spinach Egg
    Scramble, 88
  Quick and Simple Sautéed
    Spinach, 123
  Turkey Loaf, 90
Spiritual health, 28–29
Spouses, 19
Squash. *See* Winter squash; Zucchini
Starch. *See* Resistant starch
Stevia, 53–54
Stew, Crock Pot, 83
Storage containers for food, 57
Stoves, gas/propane, 56

Strawberries
  Frozen Fruit Bowl, 168
  Strawberries & Cream, 146
  Strawberry & Coconut Milk
    Smoothie, 181
  Strawberry and Banana Split
    Parfait, 153
Stress, emotional, 27–28
Stuffed Cabbage Rolls, Beef, 103
Sugar, 17
  See also Cravings and addiction
  food labels and, 57–58
  forms of, 3, 63
  in fruit, 10–11
  holidays and, 32–38
  stevia, 53–54
Sunflower Dipped Banana Bites, 140
Sunflower Macaroons, 144
Sunflower oil, 51
Sunlight, 32
Support system, 20–21
Sweeteners. *See* Sugar
Sweet or Spicy Butter Balls,
  132–133
Sweet Potato, I'm in Nirvana,
  128–129
Sweet potatoes, 2, 4

Tangerines, 47
Tea, avoiding, 15–16
Tea, Herbal Iced, 186
Thumbprint Cookies, All-Purpose
  No-Bake, 149–150
Tis the Season Smoothie, 184
Tomatoes, 12
Toxins, 27, 54
Travel. *See* Eating out
Truvia, 54
Turkey
  Basic Roasted Turkey Breast, 69
  Southwestern Turkey Burger, 82
  Turkey Loaf, 90
Tyramine foods, high, 7–8

Underweight, 13

Valentine's Day, 35–37
Vanilla Almond Butter, 142–143
Vanilla Bean Banana "Ice Cream,"
    163–164
Vanilla Drops, 155
Vanilla Pudding, 169–170
Vegetable juice, as dye for coloring
    eggs at Easter, 60
Vegetables
    See also Salads; Side dishes;
        Specific vegetable
    avoiding, as snack, 55
    Beef & Veggie Wraps, 78–79
    boiling vs. steaming, 9, 59
    canned, 57
    carb content, by type, 191–192
    carb intake, daily, 2
    complex carbohydrates, 17
    cooked vs. raw, 42–43, 191
    Cornish Hen and Vegetables, 107
    Crock Pot Stew, 83
    frozen vs. fresh, 60
    high-carb, paleo approved, 2, 4,
        42
    high FODMAPs, 9–11
    high glutamate, 8
    high histamine/tyramine, 6–8
    high oxalate, 9
    nightshade family, 12
    planning meals, 22, 64–68
    SIBO and, 11–12
    Simple Roast with Vegetables, 92

    types to eat/avoid, 62–63
Vinegar, 42, 43, 60

Walnuts, 6, 8, 48–49
Water, 15–16, 53, 57
Weight management, 12–13, 46
Whipped Cream, Dairy-Free,
    135–136
Whipped Cream, The Real Deal, 137
Whole grains, 3–4, 17, 63
Winter squash, 2, 4, 42, 72
Women, postmenopausal, 12, 46
Wrap, Mexican Paleo, 94–95
Wraps, Beef & Veggie, 78–79

Yellow Squash & Zucchini,
    Roasted, 134
Yogurt, 3, 6, 10
    candida population, health risks
        for, 52–53
    Greek yogurt, 52
    Holiday Nog, 185
    Vanilla Pudding, 169–170

Zucchini
    Pasta-Free Spaghetti in Meat
        Sauce; variation, 72
    as replacement for pasta, 59
    Roasted Zucchini & Yellow
        Squash, 134
    Simple Zucchini Soup, 124
    Zucchini Noodle and Sausage
        Casserole, 110
    Zucchini Noodles, 114–115

Printed in the USA
CPSIA information can be obtained
at www.ICGtesting.com
JSHW012027140824
68134JS00033B/2915